© No part of this book may be reproduced without permission of
JC Graphics
Thamesford, Ontario, Canada

Edited and Compiled by: Linda J Speck Schwientek

Thumbs Up Publications

Printed in Canada

ISBN: 978-0-9936318-3-2

Published 2018

Thank You

JC Graphics would like to
acknowledge & thank
Lisa Teeple of the Township of Zorra
for all her help in compiling this book.

What story does your Family Tree tell?

2016 Headlines

Royal Tour

News organizations, entertainment publications and gossip columns from around the world closely followed every step of the Cambridge's royal tour in Canada in September.

Prince William and his wife Catherine brought along their two children Prince George, 3, and Princess Charlotte, 1, on the 8 day visit throughout B.C. and the Yukon. It was the first official trip for Princess Charlotte and photographers were itching to snap some shots of the newest royal.

Of course, the children weren't the only highlights of the visit. The Duchess of Cambridge's fashion choices were also the subject of intense scrutiny. The Telegraph's headline revealed their focus of the visit, "Every outfit analysed: How the Duchess did Canada in serious high fashion style."

Fort McMurray Wildfire

The devastating Fort McMurray wildfire, which destroyed 2,400 homes and prompted the largest mass evacuation in Alberta's history, garnered international attention during the spring of 2016.

The dramatic pictures of residents fleeing the flames during the evacuation and the resulting destruction in the aftermath were widely shared around the world. At its peak, the fire nicknamed "The Beast," grew to nearly 590,000 hectares. Approximately 90,000 residents were displaced during the fire and the Insurance Bureau of Canada estimated the cost of the damage from the fire at $3.58 billion.

Canadian immigration website overwhelmed

On November 8, as the results of the U.S. presidential election began to roll in and then-candidate Donald Trump's victory became increasingly apparent, the Canadian immigration website experienced a surge of unexpected activity. The surge was so great that the website crashed that evening and users were no longer able to access the site.

In the days following, Immigration, Refugees and Citizenship Canada confirmed that the spike came from more than 200,000 users visiting the site that evening, approximately 50% had American IP addresses. The story made headlines accompanied by stories on how desperate Americans were wanting flee the U.S. and a Trump presidency.

2017 Headlines

Pineapple on Pizza?

The Greek migrant who says he first put one of the most controversial toppings on a pizza died in June at 83 in London, Ontario. Sam Panopoulos says he created the Hawaiian pizza in 1962 in Chatham, Ontario.

Legal Pot

Canada's move to legalize recreational marijuana use by July 2018 got plenty of worldwide attention.

Canada will become only the 2nd nation after Uruguay to completely legalize marijuana as a consumer product. Each province will govern how the drug will be distributed and sold.

Between 4-6 million Canadians will use cannabis recreationally next year, Health Canada estimates.

Happy Birthday Canada!

Canada celebrated its 150th birthday with a year-long nationwide patriotic party, culminating in a July 1 bash in Ottawa, which included a performance by Irish rockers U2.

"When others build walls, you open doors; when others divide, your arms are open wide; where you lead, others follow," lead singer Bono said.

"Canada is a country made strong not in spite of our differences but because of them," Prime Minister Justin Trudeau told the gathering.

CANADA 150

Sixties Scoop

Canada's $750-million settlement with victims of the Sixties Scoop, in which indigenous children were forcibly taken from their families and put up for adoption by non-Native families in Canada and around the world, made headlines. The settlement — affecting as many as 30,000 people — is part of a broader push across Canada in the last few years to grapple with its legacy of injustices against the country's indigenous populations.

ZORRA TOWNSHIP

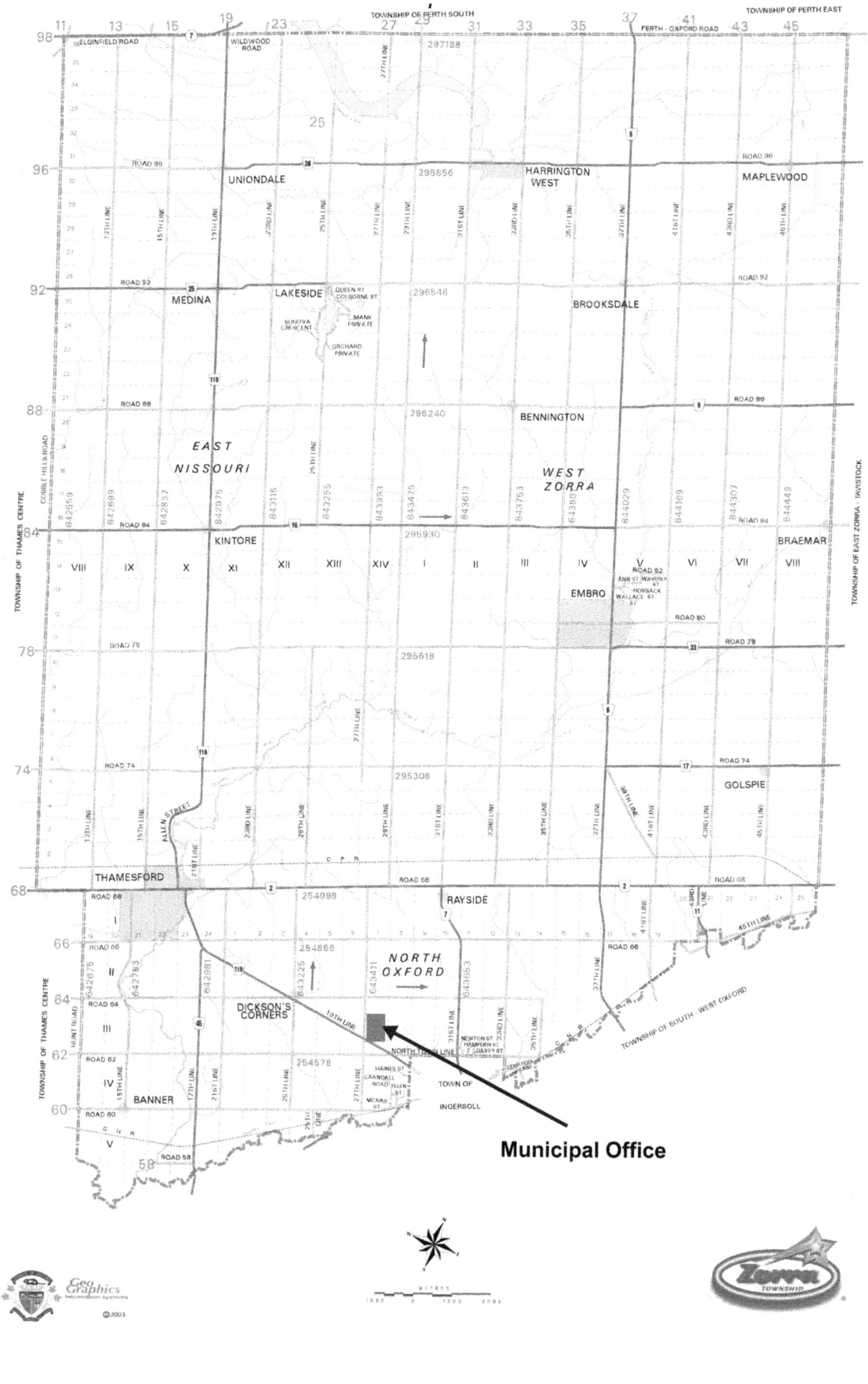

Municipal Office

Table of Contents

Family Stories
- Bennett 9
- Hammond 11
- McKellar 12
- Reavely 15
- Sutherland 18

Sports 21

Zorra Township 26

Embro 61

Thamesford 66

Kintore 81

Harrington 82

Military 89

Schools 95

Agriculture 98

The Township of Zorra is a rural municipality within the County of Oxford.

The Township is comprised of several rural clusters and two serviced villages.

The population of Zorra Township is 8,138, with a total land area of 529 square kilometres.

Family Stories

BENNETT FAMILY
Lot 8, Concession 1

John Bennett was born in England in 1812 and immigrated to Canada.

On October 17, 1939 in the District of Brock, he married Hannah Chamberlain (1820-1862) of New York State.

John & Hannah had 4 children: Ann, 1841-1875 (married William W Allen and moved to Smith's Creek, Port Huron, Michigan; died at age 34); Mary, 1844-1862 (died at age 18 on the same day as her mother); Oliver, 1847-1848; William Wallace, 1849-1913 (married Lucy Catherine Harris of Lot 7, Con. 2 on April 28, 1874; by 1891 they had moved to British Columbia).

In 1846 John bought the east half of Lot 8, Concession 1 in West Zorra. The family lived in a log house but sometime between 1852 and 1861 a 1½ storey fieldstone house was built and it is still there.

On January 28, 1862 John's wife, Hannah and their second daughter, Mary died.

John remarried on March 31, 1863. His wife was Emmaline Reavely of East Nissouri (born February 27, 1837). Emmaline's son, Frank, born May 29, 1858 was given John's surname. On July 19, 1882 in Thessalon, Frank married Laura Hotchkiss of Elgin County. They lived in Thessalon and had 10 children. Frank Reavely Bennett died from Typhoid Fever in December 1907 at the age 49.

John & Emmaline had 3 children. Their first son, Frederick "Fred" Clarence was born on August 23, 1865 and eventually took over the farm. Their second son, John A. born on November 15, 1867 died on February 12, 1870 at the age of 2 years and 3 months. Daughter Clara Blanche was born on December 6, 1870.

In 1886 Emmaline & John became the guardians of Mary "May" Ethel Wilde after her mother, Annie (née Reavely) Wilde died. Annie was the daughter of Emmaline's brother, Amos Bears Reavely Jr. On March 19, 1913, in Embro Village, May married Hugh Anderson Sutherland of Lot 6, Concession 2.

Clara & Fred Bennett with their cousin Mary "May" Ethel Wilde.

John Bennett died at home on April 4, 1890 at age 78. He had been paralysed for 7 years.

John willed the east half of Lot 8, Con. 1 and the Cedar lot (12½ acres) on the east part of Lot 5, Con. 6 to his wife Emmaline. Upon her death this property would be passed onto her son, Frederick. The 3 lots he owned in the town of Ingersoll lying on Oxford Avenue were left to his son William Wallace. He bequeathed money to his daughter Clara and his grandson, John Bennett Allen (only child of his deceased daughter, Annie).

Emmaline died on June 21, 1919 and the farm was passed onto her son, Fred.

Emmaline (Reavely) Bennett & her sister with Clara (Bennett) Karn, May Wilde & Fred Bennett

Fred lived continuously on the farm where he was born. He never married. He was widely known in the community. From 1906-1908 he was a Councillor for the Township of West Zorra. He was a life member of Thistle Masonic Lodge, No. 250 A.F. & A.M., Embro and also a life member of Harris Chapter, No. 41, R.A.M., Ingersoll. After a long illness Fred died on April 14, 1945.

On February 25, 1907 Clara married Howard Karn (son of George Karn & Eliza Ann Bullis). They lived on the Bennett farm. They had no children. Howard died on February 19, 1926 and Clara died on May 15, 1942.

Bennett family home

Fred Bennett plowing the field beside the Bennett's fieldstone house

HAMMOND FAMILY
Lot 2 Concession 2, West Zorra Township

The Hammond family of Lot 2 Concession 2, West Zorra Township were descendants of William Hammond (1871-1958) who was a Home Child and Sarah Hansford (1871-1970). William and Sarah were married March 6, 1893 in the tollbooth run by Sarah's mother on the Culloden Road, near Banner, Ontario. Following their marriage, they rented farms in West Oxford Township and Lot 6 Concession 1 West Zorra Township before purchasing a farm in Banner, Ontario. William and Sarah had seven children, Gordon, Ross, Lena, Oliveen, Wilburn, Harley and Stanley. William and Sarah are interred in Banner Cemetery, North Oxford Township.

Their son, Ross Hammond (1897-1995) and Elsie Innes (1899-1980) were married June 23, 1920 in Harrington, Ontario by Rev. A. D. Cornett. Elsie was the daughter of William Innes and Ellen (Nell) Shelley of Brooksdale, Ontario. After their marriage, they rented the farm at Lot 3 Concession 14 East Nissouri Township. In 1926, they purchased the north half of Lot 2 Concession 2, West Zorra Township and raised their son, William and daughter Helen on this farm. The northeast quarter was sold to Canada Cement in 1955 and the northwest quarter less 1-1/2 acres was sold to Martin and Anna Kirwin in 1972. Ross and Elsie resided in the home on the severed lot until their deaths. They are interred in North Embro Cemetery.

Ross and Elsie Hammond Wedding

William and Sarah Hammond Wedding

*Helen and Bill Hammond
Circa 1940*

McKELLAR FAMILY

Duncan McKellar (1831-1908) the son of John McKellar and Mary McArthur emigrated in 1847 from Kilmichael, Argyllshire, Scotland. In 1866 he married Ann McArthur (1844-1918) the daughter of Janet McDonald and Donald McArthur of Lot 11 Concession 12 East Nissouri Township. They raised a family of seven children and resided in both West Zorra and East Nissouri Township.

See McKellar story in "East Nissouri Township: People, Perseverance, Progress" Volume 2, Pages 825-830.

Donald McKellar

Margaret (Weir) McKellar

Ann (McArthur) McKellar

Ann and Duncan's oldest son, Donald (1868-1943) and Margaret Weir (1872-1960), the fifth daughter of Grantina Sutherland and George Weir were married by Rev. John Lindsay on April 6, 1904 in the Presbyterian Manse at Kintore.

Following their marriage, Donald and Margaret settled on Lot 16 Concession 7 West Zorra Township. Their first three children were born on this farm, Iola (1905-1986), Kenneth (1907- 2003) and Grant (1909-1958).

In 1911, they moved to the Weir farm to live with Margaret's brother Thomas Weir at Lot 8 Concession 12 East Nissouri Township and three more children were added to their family, Marion (1911-1908) and Murray (1911-2004) who were twins and Elizabeth 1913-1977).

Donald and Margaret raised their family on the farm on Concession 12 and they continued to live there until Donald's death in 1943.

Margaret and Donald McKellar
Golden Years

McKellar Home Lot 16 Concession 7 West Zorra
Margaret McKellar holding daughter Iola, Donald McKellar and
Margaret's mother, Grantina (Sutherland) Weir.

Weir-McKellar Homestead Lot 8 Concession 12 Home, Early 1900's

Left: William and Jean (McKellar) Hammond
Right: Verne and Helen (Hammond) Barnim - 2003

Former Hammond Home and Barn
Lot 2 Concession 2 West Zorra Township in 2009

See Hammond story in "East Nissouri Township: People, Perseverance, Progress, Page 697 Volume 2, published 2012.

REAVELY FAMILY
Lot 6, Concession 9, East Nissouri

Amos Bears Reavely's journey to Lot 6, Concession 9 in East Nissouri was started by his father Theophilus in 1801 and took more than 50 years to complete.

Theophilus Reavely was born in February 25, 1779 in Northumberland, England. Seeking work Theophilus and some of his relatives moved to Edinburgh, Galashiels, Selkirk, Scotland. While working in that town, Theophilus met Isabel Renwick. On May 3, 1800 they married in New Greyfriar's Parish, Galashiels, Edinburgh. Their son Mark was born in Galashiels on August 8 of that same year. The following spring Theophilus & Isabel sailed to America with their young child and Isabel's parents.

A dyer by trade, Theophilus travelled through New York State and set up carding mills.

Theophilus & Isabel had four sons: Mark (1800-1857), Walter (1810-1878), Amos Bears (1811-1870) and John. They also had four daughters: Henrietta, Elizabeth "Eliza" (1806-1882), Mary and Margaret (born 1816). Their children settled in various parts of Ontario.

The Reavely family came to Canada circa 1820 and settled in the Niagara region. Theophilus established one of the earliest woolen mills at St. Catherines. About 1833 their daughter Elizabeth married George Reece and lived in Pelham, Welland County. Her younger sister Margaret also chose to remain in that area and lived with Elizabeth and her family. It was here that their son, Mark met & married Jemima Osterhout. Mark farmed in Windham, Norfolk County.

Amos Bears Reavely was born on September 27, 1811 in Delhi, Delaware in New York State. After his father moved the family to Norwich Amos met Eleanor Mansfield who had also been born in New York State on January 7, 1812 in Genesee Valley. On May 15, 1833 Amos and Eleanor married. That same year Amos' brother Walter married Eleanor's sister, Theodaty. Walter and Theodaty remained in South Norwich and farmed there.

Shortly after their marriage Amos and Eleanor settled in Windham, Norfolk County. They had 11 children: Thomas, 1834-1913 (married Jane McKone abt. 1859; farmed in both East & West Nissouri; retired to London, Ontario); Emmaline, 1937-1919 (married John Bennett of Lot 8, Con.1 in West Zorra on Mar. 31, 1863); Isabella, 1838-1911 (married George Walker Jr of Lot 5, Con.2, West Zorra on Dec. 16, 1863); Malinda 1840-1920 (married Mark Chalcraft of West Zorra about 1869; lived in: East Nissouri, Petersville, Adelaide & Brant); Amos Bears Jr, 1842-1865 (married Mary Godfrey on Nov. 11, 1863); Sara Jane, 1845-1921 (married Christopher Bartindale on Dec. 29, 1875; lived on Lot 24, Con.5 in North Oxford); John (born June 24, 1846-died before 1851); Theophilus, 1848-1908 (married Dorothy Ann Carter of East Nissouri on Jan. 1, 1870); George Hamilton, 1851-1935 (married Catherine Ann McLeod of East Nissouri; farmed here); Alice 1857-1936 (twin to Dennis; married Arthur Webb in 1890 in Illinois; married Frank Van Brocklin abt. 1918 in Wisconsin); Dennis, 1857-1929 (twin to Alice; married Alice Johnson of Bruce County on Feb. 5, 1880; lived in East Nissouri)

Reavely's frame house taken during a family gathering. Amos' daughter Emmaline (Reavely) Bennett is sitting on steps with relatives and neighbours

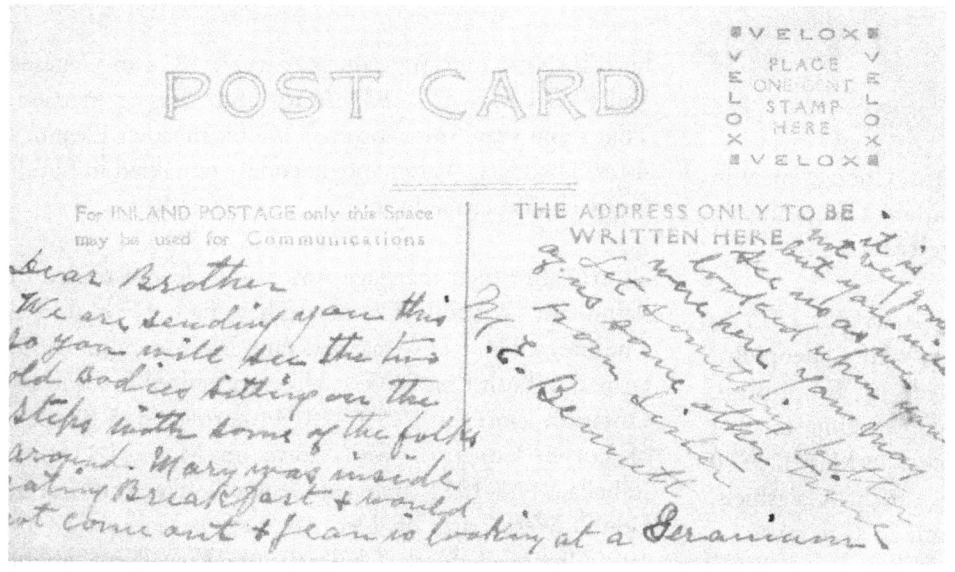

Note written by Emmaline on back of the previous photo

In the 1852 Census Amos' father, Theophilus and Eleanor's parents, John & Catherine Mansfield are living with them.

By 1857 Amos had moved his family to East Nissouri. They lived in a frame house on the east half of Lot 6, Concession 9. Amos' father Theophilus moved back to the Niagara region to live with his daughter Elizabeth. On November 13, 1857, Amos & Eleanor's twins, Alice & Dennis were born.

Amos was a member of the School Board.

On April 22, 1865 at age 23 Amos' son Amos Bears Junior was killed by the falling of a bent leaving behind his wife Mary and their eight month old daughter Annie. Annie also died young at age 22 leaving behind a two year old daughter, Mary Ethel Wilde. Mary Ethel was raised by Amos Bears Senior's daughter Emmaline (Reavely) Bennett on Lot 8, Con.1 in West Zorra. In 1913 Mary Ethel Wilde married Hugh Anderson Sutherland of Lot 6, Concession2.

Amos Bears died on September 20, 1870. He willed his land to his two sons Hamilton & Theophilus. Hamilton received the north east quarter and Theophilus received the south east quarter. Included in his bequeaths to family members he wrote: "It is also my wish that my beloved wife Eleanor Reavely shall be accommodated with a house of the old homestead with my son George Hamilton Reavely and shall have use of two Milch cows, six sheep and two pigs free from any charges whatsoever so long as she remains my widow."

Theophilus sold his share and moved to Elgin County where he was a Hotel Keeper. He later moved to Woodstock and died on January 30, 1908.

On April 13, 1882 Hamilton married Catherine Ann McLeod (1857-1928) who was an infant when her parents emigrated from Scotland. Hamilton and Catherine had two children, Ethel Renwick and George.

Their daughter, Ethel was born on June 17, 1884. In 1908 she graduated from Victoria Hospital Training School for Nurses and worked as a Registered Nurse. For a number of years she was a supervisor of nurses at Wellesley Hospital in Toronto. Later she returned home and worked as a nurse in Thamesford. Ethel died on July 2, 1933.

Their son George was born on September 20, 1888. He helped his father with the farming. Sometime during the early 1930s he married Florence (née Cook) Appleton. Florence died on February 27, 1938. George died in 1967.

On March 6, 1895 Amos' wife, Eleanor died.

By 1911 Hamilton and his family had left this farm and were living on Lot 5, Concession 10 in East Nissouri. In 1929 Hamilton's wife Catherine died.

On April 5, 1935 Hamilton died at home on Lot 5, Concession 9 in East Nissouri which was located across the road from their original homestead in East Nissouri.

> Nissouri
>
> Annie Isabella Reavely
> was Born The 14 Day
> of August in the
> year of our Lord 1864
>
> Amos Bears Reavely Junr
> was Killed by the
> falling of a Bent
> The 22 Day of April 1865

Family note: Annie Reavely's birth and Amos Bears Reavely Jr's death.

> The Anual Meeting in persuant to Publick Notice was held at the School house in Section No 5 in East Nissouri on the 14th Day of January 1857 Elmen Day Chairman Mooved Seconded and caried that William Obryan Serve in place of John Judge ▮▮▮▮▮▮ Mooved and Seconded and caried that the Teachers Salery and all other Necessary expences for the School to Be Raised By a tax on all the Ratiable property in the Said Scool Section
>
> I hereby Sertify that this is a true Statement of the precedings of the above mentioned School Meeting Sined By me Amos Reavely Sectery of Said meeting

Minutes of Annual School Board Meeting at No. 5, East Nissouri in 1857-Amos Reavely (secretary)

SUTHERLAND FAMILY
Lot 6, Concession 2

On July 8, 1852 James Sutherland bought the west half of Lot 6, Concession 2 in West Zorra (originally part of the British government's Clergy Reserves) and his descendants have lived on the farm for 162 years.

James was born in Sutherlandshire abt. 1792. On March 11, 1825 he married Ann Gray (born 1808) in Clyne, Sutherlandshire, Scotland.

They had 3 children while living in Clyne: Hugh, born 1825; Janet, born 1827; Helen, born 1829.

James and Ann immigrated to Canada with their young family in 1830. Children born after their arrival in Ontario were: Georgina, born 1833 (married William Abernethy in 1871 and lived on Lot 10, Concession 1; Georgina moved to Embro after William's death), Daniel, born Feb. 27, 1934 (married Catharine Jessop of Ingersoll and farmed here); James G, 1837-1916 (married Margaret McPherson in 1870 and farmed on Lot 24, Con. 12, East Nissouri); Ellen, born 1840 (married Ebenezer Sutherland of Lot 16, Concession 6 in 1866; they lived in Listowel) and Margaret, 1842-1904 (married J. Anderson).

James died at home on December 26, 1857 and left the farm to his wife, Ann. On December 22, 1863 Ann died and her son Daniel took over the farm.

Five years later on May 27, 1868 Daniel married Catherine Jessop of Ingersoll. They had eight children: William born 1869 (crippled by arthritis lived on the farm all his life; never married); Richard "Dick" born 1871 (married Nellie O'Melia in 1896; worked as a Master Mechanic in Detroit, Michigan); George, born 1873 (moved to Manitoba and married Mary Jane Malcolm in 1910); James "Jim" born 1875 (married Anna B. Sangster in 1905 in Hartney, Manitoba; lived in Pontiac, Michigan; worked as an landscaper); Daniel Osker, 1877-1925 (married Jessie Cleave in 1906 in Cameron, Manitoba; lived in Woodstock); Alice, 1880-1956 (married Thomas Glenworth Paterson in 1904 and lived on Lot 1, Concession 3); Anna, 1883-1956 (married George Gibson in 1911 and moved to Collingwood, Ontario) and Hugh, born Feb. 3, 1885 (married May Wilde of Lot 8, Concession 1 in 1913 and farmed here).

All of Daniel's children attended Walker's School (S.S. No.1, West Zorra) which was just down the road from their house.

Daniel's wife, Catherine (born August 12, 1845) died on September 23, 1906. Daniel died 6 years later on December 7, 1912. Daniel's youngest child, Hugh Anderson Sutherland inherited the farm.

On March 19, 1913 Hugh married his childhood classmate Mary "May" Ethel Wilde in the village of Embro. May was born February 26, 1884 in Au Sable, Michigan. She was raised by Emmaline (Reavely) & John Bennett, after her mother (Emmaline's niece, Annie Reavely) died in 1886.

Hugh and May had two children: Catherine Emmalene born July 30, 1919 and Carl Bruce born August 11, 1923. Both Catherine & Carl attended Walker's School.

In August of 1939, having just turned 16, Carl took his dad's Ford Model T and headed to the CNE in Toronto with his four friends: Don Mattson, John Murray, Don Cary and Earl Schwartz to take in the largest fair in the country. They stayed overnight and the four boys slept in the Model T in the parking lot at the CNE grounds.

Hugh, Annie, Jim, Alice & Dan Sutherland

On March 13, 1940 Catherine married Edmund George Nelson Armstrong (1913-2000) of London in Embro. They moved to London, Ontario and had four children: Rhea, Ruth Elayne, Larry & Michael. Catherine died on February 1, 2010.

1919 Hugh, May & daughter Catherine

Through friends, Carl met a young, vivacious woman from Manchester, England named Beryl Washington. She was born on June 24, 1924 and had immigrated to Canada in 1948. They married on December 10, 1949. They lived on the farm and raised eight children: Carolyn, Susan, Pamela, David, Steven, Jody, Riath and Kimble. The 5 oldest children also attended Walker's School until it closed in 1966.

Carl's daughter Pamela always looked forward to harvest time. "Late August was always a special time. Jimmy Fleming would bring his combine to take off the crops and the neighbors would come to help. There was always a big feast while they were there. The best for us kids was the leftover cakes and pies especially the raisin pie our mom, Beryl would make. In the spring we would patiently wait for the rhubarb so Granny May could make her famous rhubarb pudding and custard sauce. In the fall when we had the apple orchard we would collect the fallen apples and take them to Charlie Foster's house to have them made into cider. We would also climb and play in the orchard in the spring and summer."

The children helped with the chores. When Jessie Sutherland (Carl's Uncle Daniel's wife) came out to the farm she would always tease Carl's young son David about how to milk a cow. She would ask him, "Do you crank the tail?" David would try to explain to her how it was really done but as his parents didn't allow their children to say the word that would describe that part of the cow, he found it very difficult to tell her how a cow was milked.

Catherine's daughter, Elayne spent many holidays on the farm. She remembers playing baseball in the cow pasture with her cousins. The first time the ball landed on a cow paddy and broke through the crusty surface there was a big dispute as to who would retrieve it. Someone came up with the idea of using a large burdock leaf to wipe the ball. It worked and the game continued!

On March 2, 1962 Hugh died and the farm was left to his wife, May. Eleven years later on November 19, 1973 May died and Carl who had been farming there inherited the farm.

Most of the farm was sold to William Fleming in 1971 but the Sutherlands kept the house and 1 acre. Carl then worked in construction on a lot of different projects in Southern Ontario. In his later years he took to raising Gladiolus. He had regular customers and also sold them to people for Decoration Days at local cemeteries. He was known by many as Glad Man.

Sutherland Farm in 2004

1925 Catherine & Carl Sutherland on the farm

In 1990 Carl & Beryl's youngest child, Kimble made history as the first New Democrat from Oxford to win a seat in the legislature. At age 24 he was also Ontario's youngest MPP.

Carl's wife, Beryl died on March 4, 1999. They had been married for almost 50 years.

Carl's death on February 26, 2014 marked the end of an era as the remaining portion of the Sutherland Farm was sold to Rebecca Fleming, the daughter of William Fleming who purchased the farmland in 1971.

Carl & Beryl's children moved to other areas in Oxford County. Most of them live and work in Ingersoll. Christmas would find all of them returning to the farm for Christmas dinner. As their families grew so did the Christmas feasts. Eventually the children took turns hosting the Sutherland Christmas dinner which was attended by 3 generations.

1998 Sutherland Family
Front Row (left to right): Heather, Nick, Josh, Ryan, Brian (Petrie).
Middle Row: Kathleen (Harrison), Kristy, Beryl (Washington), Carl, Jennifer, Tara (Petrie).
Back Row: Tish (Purdy), Jody, Jennifer (Kent), Susan, Riath, Candice (Hartnett), David, Kimble, Gary (Petrie), Tom (Harrison), Carolyn, Liz (Brown), Bill (Harrison), Steven & Pamela.

Sports

Ohio Exchange

Forty-one years ago a team from Kent, Ohio was playing a tournament in Stratford and on their way home, Mother Nature unleashed a blizzard upon the region that not only shut down local businesses and highways' but made the journey back to Ohio impossible. With no other options' the friendly families in Embro opened their doors and their hearts by taking families into their homes to seek shelter from the elements. The weekend was an experience that was talked about for months that followed. Many of the families remained in contact with their new friends from Ohio well beyond the completion of the hockey season. The next hockey season brought an invitation from the Cyclones organization to Embro to continue the relationship by opening doors for a visit from Embro. Since 1977, our organizations have taken turns making the 6 hour journey across the border to share in the common love for the game of hockey and a friendship with new friends from a different country. The true joy in this event is "billeting" of the young hockey players. The annual weekend includes games played by players ranging from 7 years of age and up to 14 years of age and also includes a spirited coach's game. The weekend concludes on Sunday with a presentation of the respective countries flags and an on ice closing ceremony.

*The experience is a
lifetime memory for all those involved.*

Dunn's Softball Team

The Girls' Softball Team of Dunn's community was organized in 1920. The team is featured in From Forest to Farm: The Story of North Oxford Township (2015). These images, from the collection of Beachville District Museum, offer more information about how the team practiced and competed. Games were played at Dunn's Cheese Factory. The owner of the factory, Evan Mackenzie, was the manager of the team. He drove players to tournaments (both across the County and in London) on the back of his truck.

Dunn's Softball Team
Pictured [Left to Right]: Grace Brown, Jack Prier, Evan McKenzie, Rose Barnes, Helen Gerrie, Marjorie Nichols [?], Lil Brown, Ethel Barnes, Lauretta Oliver, Mary [?], Jim Hutson and Millie Sandick.

Dunn's softball players in action – ca. 1923
Beachville District Museum Collection, 1986.17.07.

Dunn's Softball Team headed to a tournament in Evan McKenzie's truck – ca. 1923
Beachville District Museum Collection, 1986.17.06.

Zorra Girls Hockey Assoc.
West Oxford Girls Hockey Assoc.

The Zorra Girls Hockey Association had a fantastic 2015/2016 season. Our teams competed all year in their divisions & did our community proud! Our association would like to thank the following sponsors: GOLD: Trembletts Independent. SILVER: Brent Reg Construction, Anderson Appliances, Thorndale Dental, Banner Road Vets, Thamesford Lions Club, Tim Hortons. BRONZE: Allied Associates, Vipond Fire Protection, Egan Electric, Precise Planting Services, Lori Goldhawk, Three Brydges Automotive, KDM Erectors, Brock and Visser Funeral Home, Little Caesars Woodstock, McFarlan Rowlands Insurance, Knoops Farms. COPPER: Zorra TV & Appliances, Thamesford Pizza Company, Matt Langford Insurance, Henderson Towing, Cooksville Tire, Langford Auto Care, Knoops Farm Service, Thamesford Accounting & Financial Services. Our association would also like to thank the Oxford Community Foundation and Heartland Farm Mutual (Oxford Mutual Insurance) for the grants we received this year. We were able to purchase & stock trainer bags and also purchase new much needed practice equipment for all our teams with their help! So thank you! Finally the executive would like to thank all our volunteers in our association. The coaches, trainers, managers, & dressing room volunteers who help make everything work on a daily basis. Our kids are able to play hometown hockey because of all the contributions of everyone above. That is truly an amazing thing and a testament to our great community. We hope to see everyone back for our inaugural year combined with Ingersoll Girls Hockey as West Oxford Girls Hockey Association. Our initial try out dates are for BB/B and B/C teams are starting April 23. Please check the websites www.zgha.ca or www.ingersollgirlshockey.com for updated tryout dates, times & information.

Zorra Skaters at the Provincial Podium

By Laura Green

The weekend of Mar 17-19, 2017 two skaters from the Zorra Skating Club ended their competitive season on a very high note at the Skate Ontario Championships which were held in Pt Colborne. 15 year old Ella McRoberts, a grade 10 student at Huron Park SS in Woodstock was a Silver Medalist in the Silver Triathlon Lades (accumulative score, combining 3 events, Creative Skills, Interpretive & Freeskate programs). 13 year old Justine Dodd, grade 8 student at Hickson Central School, was a Gold medalist in Star 5 Men (13 & over) division. To qualify for the Skate Ontario Champions, skaters must qualify in the top 3 spots from their respective regions. Both McRoberts & Dodd won Gold in their respective divisions at the Western Ontario Star Skate Championships held in Aylmer in February. Both are coached by Debbie Roefs from Embro and Ella's choreographer is Suzanne Killing-Wood

May 2017 Village Voice

Coach Debbie Roefs is beaming with pride with her 2 stars on ice:
Silver Medalist Ella McRoberts & Gold Medalist Justine Dodd from the Zorra Skating Club at the Skate Ontario Championships.

Fire fighter training in Zorra Township 2017

Zorra Township

Newspaper clipping supplied by Joyce Day, Lakeside

This report provided by Don MacLeod, CAO, Township of Zorra

2014-2018 Council Achievements

OUR BRAND

- We take great pride in our exceptional rural lifestyle in Zorra Township, made possible by our highly engaged community and government.
- Zorra Township's location allows residents and businesses to enjoy a small village atmosphere with abundant green space, easy and fast access to big city amenities and large consumer markets.
- Zorra is highly progressive, environmentally conscious, economically strong and prosperous.
- Our highly productive rural land provides a solid foundation for successful and varied agriculture and food production in Zorra Township.

We strive to make Zorra better by doing our part. In Zorra, we take great pride in maintaining our exceptional rural lifestyle, made possible by our highly engaged community and government. Our location allows residents and businesses to enjoy a small village atmosphere with abundant green space, easy and fast access to big city amenities and large consumer markets. Zorra is progressive, environmentally conscious, economically strong and prosperous. Our highly productive rural land provides a solid foundation for successful and varied agriculture and food production. In Zorra Township, we care.

Zorra TOWNSHIP — DOING OUR PART

Mayor Margaret Lupton

Ward 1 Councillor Ron Forbes

Ward 2 Councillor Marie Keasey

Ward 3 Councillor Marcus Ryan

Ward 4 Councillor Doug Matheson

Council Achievements 2014-2018

Message from Mayor Lupton and Council

As this term of Council draws to a close, it is time to reflect and recognize the achievements accomplished during the 2014 – 2018 term of Council. This has been a very rewarding term and with the genuine cooperation of all members of Council has allowed us to oversee many successful projects and undertakings.

Of course, none of this would have been possible without the assistance of our dedicated and hard-working staff. The level of cooperation and the single-mindedness of goal achievement between Council and Township staff is one that we can all be proud of. Council would also like to recognize the invaluable contributions from all of our volunteers, Committee members and members of the public who have helped shape our community. Your participation in Township events, public meetings and open houses provides community input that we need to help guide Council in its decision-making process. We could not have accomplished as much as we did without your help.

Zorra remains one the best places to live and raise a family because our community works together to achieve our goals. From our community groups and businesses, to local schools, libraries, hockey arenas and community centres, Zorra residents are deeply committed to making our community a more livable place for everyone.

This was reflected in the adoption of our community based Strategic Plan in 2015. The values and goals of our community were captured in a document that set the focus on making a Zorra a more sustainable, liveable community. Along with being sustainable, the community needed to balance economic growth, fiscal responsibility and environmental awareness. Initiatives throughout the Plan also focused on cultivating partnerships, engaging the community, excelling in service delivery and incorporating green principles in decision-making. Engagement of our young people and seniors will continue to be a priority for the next term of Council. We need to focus on our future while remaining true to our past.

We are proud of our accomplishments and "doing our part" to help Zorra remain such a wonderful community.

On behalf of your 2014 – 2018 Zorra Township Council, we thank you.

Margaret Lupton
Mayor Margaret Lupton

R Forbes *Marie Keasey* *Marcus Ryan* *Doug Matheson*
Ward 1 Councillor Ward 2 Councillor Ward 3 Councillor Ward 4 Councillor
Ron Forbes Marie Keasey Marcus Ryan Doug Matheson

 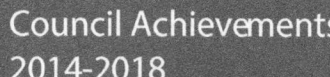

Council Achievements 2014-2018

New Council, New Visions

Shortly after the 2014 Election, Council and Staff were asked to prepare a list of ideas, goals, objectives, projects, buildings, etc. they would like to see accomplished over the term of this Council. The ideas and thoughts were wide-ranging and provided valuable input on the collective vision from Council and Staff on the future of the Township. Members of the public were also asked for input on what they would like to see accomplished over the term of Council.

In review of the goals and objectives, it became clear that Township Council was focused on long-term strategic planning. The discussion and debate that took place mimicked a typical strategic planning process without the formality or substantive public input. At that point, Council decided it was the appropriate time to consider enshrining a mission statement, vision and key principles and then refine specific goals to set the direction of the Township in its day to day operations. A set of specific strategic objectives were then developed which underwent public consultation to provide assistance to Council in defining a mission statement, vision and key principles.

What started out as a goal setting exercise morphed into a community based strategic plan that established a vision, mission, values and goals for the Township of Zorra.

The mission is for Zorra to be "A vibrant, prosperous, engaged and environmentally conscious community that evokes pride in residents for its accomplishments and continuing resilience as it forges the future".

For the remainder of this term, key initiatives and undertakings were tested against the Strategic Plan to ensure what was being proposed met the spirit and intent of the Plan.

This also led to Council undertaking a branding exercise to build upon the excellent work that led the creation of the Strategic Plan. In 2017, Zorra Township Council decided that a branding exercise was necessary in Zorra. The goals were to establish Zorra Township as a desirable destination for possible residents and visitors and to strengthen and update visual identity.

As part of this exercise, the Township identified the following needs:

- New tag line (new positioning line)
- Communications standards guide
- Community entrance signs
- Promotional items

Working closely with Karen Sample and her team at 31st Line Strategic Communications, the new brand was created and was officially launched at the December 19, 2017 Council meeting, with several community and staff members present.

After a successful launch the brand has taken off with Council, staff and the public embracing our new brand. In 2018 the Township installed 14 new gateway signs to welcome visitors to Zorra.

2015-2018 Strategic Plan

Our Vision
"A vibrant, prosperous, engaged and environmentally conscious community that evokes pride in residents for its accomplishments and continuing resilience as it forges the future"

Our Mission
"The Zorra team of elected officials, staff and volunteers works together responsibly and transparently to realize and sustain the community's vision."

Our Values

Trust - The trust between community members is what makes Zorra an inclusive community. Community trust is built through sensible planning, reliable services and public engagement.

Respect - The residents of Zorra come from diverse backgrounds. It is through respect for the varied backgrounds and experiences that common ground can be achieved.

Innovation - Zorra must be a community which embraces change. It must remain open to all ideas to become a flexible, progressive municipality which can successfully anticipate and adapt to changing environments.

Accountability - Council and staff must be accountable to Zorra residents and be responsible for actions and inactions.

Teamwork - We will work cooperatively at all levels of the organization and community to accomplish the Township's objectives and to provide our residents with quality service.

Transparency - We will conduct all affairs for the Township openly and with complete transparency, except where prohibited by law.

Our Goals

We are a *vibrant community* that values our uniqueness, creativity and takes pride in calling Zorra home.

We are a *prosperous community* that provides opportunities to work and shop in our community and to grow in a sustainable manner.

We are an *engaged community* that values all members and actively encourages involvement, engagement, openness and transparency.

We are an *environmentally conscious community* that are good stewards of our natural environment and we protect our environment by valuing our natural assets and using our resources wisely.

Renewing our Infrastructure

Thamesford Spray Pad and Skateboard Park

What started out as a vision for a few Thamesford and area residents three years ago, turned into reality a few short weeks ago with the opening of Thamesford Spray Pad and Skate Board Park. Committee Chair, Don Weir and members, Wendi Jackson, Bronwen Metcalf, Amanda Breen-Cowan, Andrew McClure, Councillor Marie Keasey and staff resource, Stephanie Starchuck worked tirelessly to see this project come to fruition. Matthew Paul, By-law Enforcement Officer/Building Inspector, was the project manager and helped this project meet deadlines and budget. With the support of Council in the form of a $150,000 contribution to the project, the Committee worked diligently to secure a $150,000 Ontario Trillium Grant and $50,000 donations from the Thamesford Lions Club, Vito Frijia of Southside Construction and Bill Loyens/Vito Frijia of Toil Development Inc. In addition, the Thamesford and area community contributed almost $110,000 in corporate and private donations.

Hogg Construction of Thamesford recently completed construction of this $525,000 project.

Council Chamber Renewal

In order to improve accessibility for members of the public attending Council meetings, a new layout with enhanced audio visual capabilities was completed in 2018. Council agendas and supporting documents are readily accessible from all areas of the Council Chamber.

Embro Soccer Pitch

The Township was approached by representatives from various soccer associations in Embro with a proposal to construct a full-sized dedicated soccer pitch on the grounds of Embro Zorra Community Centre.

In coordination with Zorra's Recreation and Facilities Department a two-year project saw a fully irrigated regulation sized soccer pitch created at the south-east corner of the grounds. The addition of this pitch will allow for greater flexibility in the use of grounds for Embro Fair, Weinerfest and possibly Embro Highland Games. Wayne and Carol Fraser donated material for this project from a residential subdivision in Embro.

Council Achievements 2014-2018

Developing Responsibly

Rooftop Solar Projects

The Township was approached by ERTH Corporation to determine if the Township was interested in partnering for the installation of rooftop solar panels at Thamesford District Recreation Centre and Embro Zorra Community Centre. ERTH applied for these projects under the Feed In Tariff 4 program under the Green Energy Act. ERTH was awarded the contracts and presented a proposal to Council to rent space from the municipality for a period of 20 years in return for annual rent payments of $17,000.

Electric Vehicle Charging Stations

The Workplace Electric Vehicle Charging Incentive Program (WEVCIP) was announced in early 2018 to support employers that wish to provide Level 2 electric vehicle chargers for their employees or workplace tenants by providing 80 per cent of the initial cost, up to $7,500 per charging space. The Township submitted an application for two charging units at the Municipal Office as this facility was the only one that met the criteria of having 10 employees at a work site location. The Township was advised the application was approved for the installation of two charging stations at the Municipal Office. Installation took place early in 2018 and both stations

have seen considerable use since they were installed.

Smart Growth

How Zorra grows and develops as a community is as important as what is built. Council and staff carefully consider development options and engage with residents and businesses to ensure Zorra continues to be a place where everyone has an opportunity to thrive.

Sustainable and smart growth are vitally important to the overall health and well being of our community and it is imperative that it be well planned. Thamesford and Embro are both designated as growth communities due to being serviced by municipal water and municipal sanitary sewage. Millions of dollars has been invested by the County of Oxford and the Township of Zorra on these municipal services and in order to minimize the amount of productive farmland lost for development purposes, compact and dense growth is desired. Council and County planning staff carefully considered subdivision applications in Embro and Thamesford and worked with the respective developers to densify growth to maximize land use. Over this term of Council there has been a total of 127 new houses constructed Township wide with the majority being built in Thamesford and Embro.

Protecting Farmland

This Council took a firm approach to a boundary adjustment with the Town of Ingersoll. The proposal was rejected by Council until such time as the needs can be justified and sustainable development practices are implemented. Council also strongly opposed the province's proposal for a high-speed rail corridor in Zorra Township.

Council Achievements 2014-2018

Dynamic, Thriving and Strong

During this term of Council, there were many other initiatives and projects that took place to make Zorra a more dynamic, vital and thriving community. Many were minor in nature, but when grouped together all helped make Zorra a stronger community.

Recreation, Arts & Culture Master Plan

In 2017, Council authorized the preparation of a Recreation, Arts & Culture Master Plan.

The Master Plan process was all encompassing and many user groups and residents were able to participate during its preparation and the consultation phase. The result of this, is a document that sets the following strategic directions:

Focus on Healthy Communities
Encourage active lifestyles, public engagement, and strong communities.

Work Together
Build capacity through continuous staff development, supporting volunteers, and seeking community partners in the delivery of parks, recreation, arts, and culture services.

Promote Awareness of Opportunities
Promote the coordinated communication of parks, recreation, arts, and culture opportunities and facilitate the sharing of information among community partners.

Keep Facilities Relevant
Commit to a high standard of facility maintenance and management, and update and renew aging facilities, as necessary, in coordination with facility users.

Enhance Parks, Open Spaces, and Trails
Be stewards of parks, open spaces, and trails to ensure that current and future generations are able to experience Zorra's natural environment.

Along with these strategic directions the report also contained 54 specific recommendations that will require significant resources over the next 10 years.

Recreation Enhancements

The Recreation and Facilities Department underwent significant changes during this past term. It was identified by Council that a more active role in program development was required in order to provide recreation activities outside of organized sports. Stephanie Starchuck was hired as the Recreation and Facilities Program Coordinator to help implement a programing component. New programs include, a summer day camp and PD day camps, as well as partnering with schools and other agencies to provide programming.

More recently, Council authorized implementation of new software to make renting our halls, arenas and sports fields easier and readily accessible for all residents.

Mayor Lupton helps Sharon at Tim Hortons Camp Day

The Tim Horton Children's Foundation is a non-profit charitable organization founded in 1974. Funding comes from Camp Day & year round donations at more than 3,700 Tim Hortons Restaurants. Since 1975, more than 150,000 children and youth have attended a Foundation camp at no cost to them or their families.

Senior of the Year 2016 Anne Hollis

Deputy Mayor Keasey presents CAO Don MacLeod with Canadian Association of Municipal Administrators 15 year pin

Chief McFarlan and Sparky at the Outdoor Farm Show

New Tanker truck at the Thamesford Fire Station

Fire Fighter Certification & Long Service Awards
March 29, 2017

Back Row (L-R): Murray Perry, John Renkema, Dave Switzer, Matt Hopkins, Paul Mitchell, Corby Kirwin, John McFarlan, Deanna Kirwin, Jim Manzer, Dennis Weaver, Matt Cockle, Chris Schurman, Tammy Spriel. Front Row (L-R): Charlie Weir, Jeff King, Mike Pickering, Steve Greason, Ron King, Bruce Brebner, Ashley Aldred, Matt Van Ginkel, Wes Crandall, Carley Crandall, Cody Brown.

NFPA Certification
NFPA 1001 (Fire Fighter I & II) includes MFPA 472 HAZMAT

EMBRO STATION
Ashlee Aldred   Carley Crandall
Wes Crandall   Deanna Kirwin

THAMESFORD STATION
Murray Perry   Tammy Spriel
Mike King   Justan Van Maar

NFPA 1041
Fire Service Instructor Level I
EMBRO STATION
Deanna Kirwin

NFPA 1006 Technical Rescuer (Chapter 5)
EMBRO STATION
Mike Belanger   Len Brown   Matt Cockle

Long Service Awards
Federal Fire Service Exemplary Service

20 YEAR MEDAL   John Renkema

30 YEAR BAR
Steve Greason   Jim Manzer   Dave Switzer
Charlie Weir   Dennis Weaver

40 YEAR BAR   Ron King

Long Service Awards   Provincial Long Service

30 YEAR BAR
Steve Greason   Jim Manzer   Dave Switzer
Charlie Weir   Dennis Weaver

35 YEAR BAR   John McFarlan   Paul Mitchell

40 YEAR BAR   Ron King

Canada 150 swag from the Township office

CAN 150 at Oxford County Library
connect. discover. share. become.

Thank You
to our sponsors!

We salute these local businesses and organizations for their support of our 2017 CAN150 programs.

   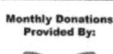 

Maple leaf collage, Tavistock summer reading club.

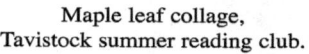

150 Library moments to celebrate Canada's 150th birthday
Summer Reading Challenge

O Canada

become.
{ Grow to be; develop into. }

share.
{ use, occupy, or enjoy something jointly with another or others. }

discover.
{ show interest in an activity or subject for the first time. }

connect.
{ form a relationship, or feel an affinity. }

CAN 150 at OCL

2017 by the Numbers

310,019 in-person visits

30,084 people attended 2,890 programs

444,113 physical items borrowed

117,457 digital items downloaded

} **561,570 TOTAL ITEMS**

98,232 public access computer sessions

285 computer coaching sessions

538 people at 51 Tech Boot Camps

16,302 Active library members

12% of users were "*POWER USERS*" borrowing at least 500 items!

26% Amazing users borrowed **100** to **499** items!

6,907 books & books on CD were delivered to home delivery clients & long term care residents.

Future Oxford's Environmental Pillar

According to the recent Canadian Index of Well-Being results in Oxford, 88% of residents feel "a personal responsibility for the environment. That's an astonishing commitment to sustainability. So, when an invitation was sent to all on a list of Oxford organizations, plus a few others whose interest in was known, the response was swift. Replies began. They included confirmations of attendance, regrets of unavailability, questions about being glad they had received the invitation, requests for the notes from the meeting, remarks about Future Oxford's actions, asking if they could bring a friend who was highly engaged too. The answer – of course! Various groups and/or individuals identified actions they were engaged in which were listed under the goals in the Community Sustainability Plan or which met the goals despite not being a listed action. It was agreed that the achievement of goals was more important than hewing to the actions listed, i.e., that the goals are important & the actions are examples, and often exemplary. We discovered a broad consensus on the goals in the environmental portion of the Future Oxford Sustainability Plan, that many actions are well under way which will contribute to the realization of those goals, and that some actions which serve the goals were not even imagined at the start of the Community Sustainability consultations. All this is good. In addition, there was significant overlap among the actions being done & planned by various groups and individuals present, meaning that we have driven our goals higher than expected. The next meeting of the Environmental Pillar of Future Oxford will include yet more groups. If your group was not represented at the initial meeting – check with your members on this – please contact Bryan Smith, the Acting Chair, at bryan-smith@oxford.net. For more information on the environmental, community & economic action consult http://www.futureoxford.ca/ or meet them April 20 at Future Oxford Expo in the Oxford Auditorium on the Woodstock Fairgrounds.

Harvey Waud Exhibit

Louise Waud and Lorne Waud at the Harvey Waud Exhibit opening, 2017.

Opening of the Harvey Waud Exhibit, Beachville District Museum, 2017

Harvey Waud was born in 1922 and raised on a farm just outside Lakeside, Ontario. In 1949, he married Margaret Wheeler and the two purchased a farm at R.R. #2, Lakeside. The couple raised 5 children and farmed there for over 40 years before retiring in Embro. Harvey had a passion for collecting farm tools and implements. He often put his pieces on display in his drive shed, sharing them with others. When he and Margaret moved to Embro, their basement on Wallace Crescent became a place where neighbours, visitors and even school groups learned about agricultural practices and local history. To celebrate the country's sesquicentennial, and the significance of Waud's collection, Beachville District Museum held its opening of the Harvey Waud Exhibit on Saturday, June 3, 2017.

150th Beachville District Museum
SATURDAY June 3
10am - 4pm
Canada Celebration Day

Come celebrate with us, everyone welcome, the Opening of the Permanent Harvey Waud Exhibit 11:00am

• 150 years of Canada Exhibit •

Petting Zoo, Goats, Ducks, Rabbits, Alpacas etc.

• 1838 Baseball games played: 11:30am and 1:30pm •

Food Booth, Hot Dogs, Burgers, Pop, Face Painting and lots more.....

Visitors to the petting zoo at Beachville District Museum during the Zorra150 event in 2017.

The Late Nineteenth-Century Stone Farm Houses of John Thompson Crellin

By Armstrong, K. E. (2018). The Late Nineteenth-century Stone Farmhouses of John Thompson Crellin. Journal of the Society for the Study of Architecture in Canada, 43(2), 27–41. https:// doi.org/10.7202/1058037ar

KAREN ARMSTRONG *is a graduate of the School of Fashion at Ryerson Institute of Technology (Ryerson University). An independent scholar, her interests are centred on nineteenth-century buildings in Ontario.*

The abundant published materials that offered design inspiration and aesthetic advice in England and the United States from the late eighteenth century onward were a major influence on nineteenth-century architecture. Recent scholarship examining house patterns published in *The Canada Farmer* between 1864 and 1876 has revealed the power of print media to shape an array of relatively modest dwellings in towns and cities in Southern Ontario. This article will show the impact of print media on rural housing in Oxford County and the role of an unknown English immigrant stonemason, John Thompson Crellin, in the translation of five designs published by James Avon Smith in *The Canada Farmer* into twelve stone farmhouses. Working between 1870 and 1891, Crellin developed a unique, instantly recognizable colour pattern on his façades derived from multi-coloured fieldstones sourced from farmers' fields. The widely disseminated ideas of the British theorist John Ruskin seem to be reflected in these farmhouses, particularly in the ways Crellin's wall construction reveals the inherent qualities of quarry-faced masonry.

A close examination of Crellin's twelve stone farmhouses shows how, over time, the stonemason and his clients evolved away from the strict implementation of the house designs from *The Canada Farmer* toward a new vision for the planning of their farmhouses. Far from being remote and isolated, the houses are evidence that the farmers were connected to the mainstream through new developments in transportation, technology, and aesthetic thought emanating from abroad and visible in sophisticated urban centres like London in Ontario. What makes this research especially potent is that by 1891 in Crellin's

John Thompson Crellin
Special thanks to Alice Crellin Ingle. Fig. 1

last known building, his patron David Lawrence appears to have believed that he invented something new, publishing an illustrated description of his house in a major American farm journal. Lawrence's foray into publishing illustrates that these farmers were keenly aware of their ties to the world and that they too could participate in the international economy of design ideas.

> **MODELS FOR INSPIRATION: JAMES AVON SMITH AND THE CANADA FARMER**
> "I desire my reader to observe carefully how much of his pleasure in building is derived, or should be derived, from admiration of the intellect of men whose names he knows not."
> - Ruskin, *The Stones of Venice.*[3]

In 1864, *The Globe* newspaper in Toronto began publishing *The Canada Farmer*, a biweekly journal. It included a column titled "Rural Architecture" in many of its issues written by the prolific Toronto based architect James Avon Smith [1832-1918]. His ideas were up-to-date and he realized that through print media he could provide readers with construction advice and helpful suggestions to guide their thinking and aesthetic choices. Over the course of roughly ten years he published designs for approximately eighteen houses, two churches, four schoolhouses, an octagonal exhibition building, and buildings for a farm of one hundred acres. Smith's articles published in *The Canada Farmer* were the only Canadian source that disseminated modern design ideas to a Canadian readership until *The Canadian Architect and Builder* appeared in 1888. The main competition was American pattern book publishing, which increased over the years; Canadians read and ordered house patterns from them. According to Harold Kalman, "Canadian architects and builders read those pattern books which must have had an immense impact on their designs, but few of the associated houses have been identified."[4]

Smith read American pattern book literature citing Andrew Jackson Downing [1815-1852] and Lewis Falley Allen [1800-1890] in some of his house descriptions. Smith agreed with Downing's statement that "a good house is a powerful means of civilization..."[5] In the same article Smith borrowed a house plan from Downing and quoted his advice: "The house should look like a farmhouse, expressing the beauty of a farmer's life..."[6] In another description, he quoted Allen who wrote: "The house should present an agreeable aspect from all viewing points..."[7] Smith's articles also reveal that he was aware of larger international trends. Another major source was the work of the prominent British theorist John Ruskin [1819-1900]. As Henry-Russell Hitchcock observed, "Ruskin had almost from the original publication of his *Seven Lamps of Architecture* in 1849 more readers beyond the seas than at home."[8] Although he does not name Ruskin, when one reads Smith's articles, Ruskin's ideas are apparent.[9] Like Ruskin, Smith prized the qualities of stone, saying: "There is... an air of stability and durability about a stone structure; age, so far from being destructive to it, only increases its beauty..."[10]

In an article published in 1869, Smith stated that "many of the designs from *The Canada Farmer* have been used as models all over the province."[11] Smith's first three elevations are discussed by Jessica Mace in her 2013 article examining vernacular nineteenth-century Gothic Revival houses in Southern Ontario. Mace has shown that Smith is responsible for more houses in Ontario than any other nineteenth-century architect, stating that his plans were "meant to be a basic and versatile prototype rather than a direct model."[12] In his examination of nineteenth-century housing in downtown Toronto, Scott Weir outlined the history and development of the bay-and-gable house style from its origins in eighteenth century England. Bay-and-gable houses appeared in Toronto from around 1870 to 1900.[13] Smith wrote in 1867: "A home similar to the above [Smith's drawing] was erected in Toronto in 1863..."[14] He illustrated that article with his flat façade story-and-a-half "Country House." It has an interior plan almost identical to the house plans illustrated in Weir's article.[15] The success of Smith's published designs in *The Canada Farmer* was due to the clarity and simplicity of his plans. They were easily adapted to stylistic changes, tightly packed building sites, and city restrictions. Best of all, the designs were available to farmers and builders for a dollar a year or eight cents a copy from the presses at the *Globe* newspaper.

A RURAL "BUILDER AND CONTRACTOR": JOHN THOMPSON CRELLIN[16]
"In no art is there closer connection between our delight in the work and our admiration of the workman's mind than in architecture, and yet we rarely ask for a builder's name."
- Ruskin, *The Stones of Venice.*[17]

As the recent articles by Mace and Weir suggest, the implementation of Smith's designs fell to the many anonymous craftsmen and clients throughout Ontario who found inspiration in *The Canada Farmer*. This article will focus on a group of twelve modest but distinctive farmhouses built by one craftsman - John Thompson Crellin - and the clientele of farmers who hired him and contributed to translating architectural diagrams into farmhouses reflecting their way of life. Crellin's stonemasonry made Smith's designs into a physical reality in the Ontario landscape. The farmhouses reveal the striking yet hitherto little-examined potential for the humble craftsman to realize the larger aesthetic goals advocated by prominent theorists such as Ruskin who inspired sophisticated urban architects like Smith. Instead of hiring an architect, Crellin's clients paid the stonemason to provide them with the good taste and sophistication that Smith hoped would transform the countryside. With their distinctive masonry, patterning, and colour, the houses examined in this article are in essence signed "John Thompson Crellin."

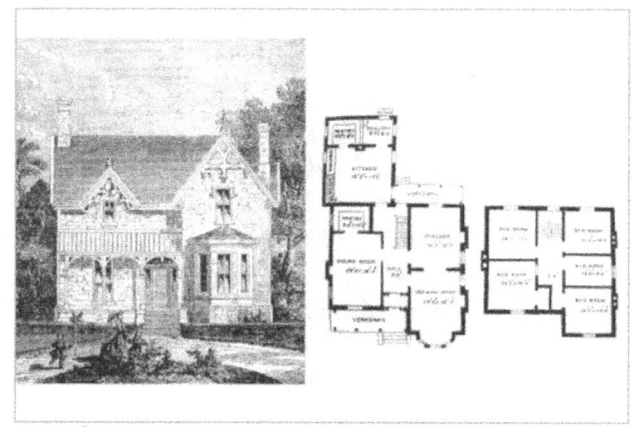

"Suburban Villa or Farm House"
The Canada Farmer, 1864, Vol. 1, No. 9, P. 132
Toronto Reference Library, Special Collections Department
Fig. 2.1

"A Cheap Country House"
The Canada Farmer, 1868, Vol. 5, No. 16, P. 244-245
Toronto Reference Library, Special Collections Department
Fig. 2.4

"A Cheap Farmhouse"
The Canada Farmer, 1864, Vol. 1, No. 24, P. 340
Toronto Reference Library, Special Collections Department
Fig. 2.2

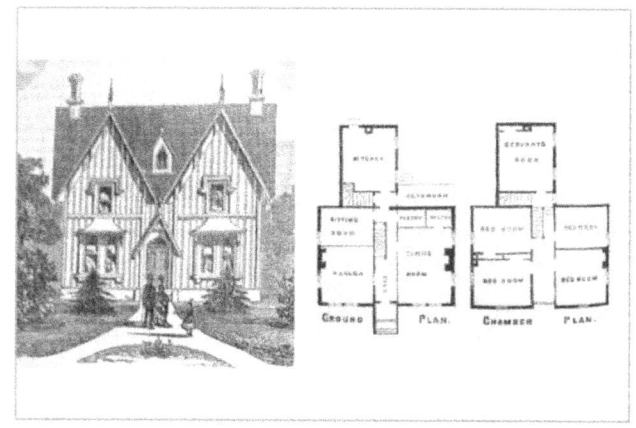

"Design of a Small Farm Dwelling"
The Canada Farmer, 1871, Vol. 3, No. 1, P. 16
Toronto Reference Library, Special Collections Department
Fig. 2.5

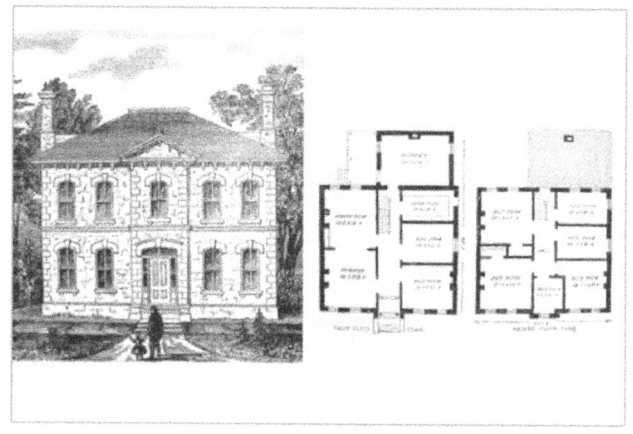

"A Two Storey Farm House"
The Canada Farmer, 1865, Vol. 2, No. 8, P. 116-117
Toronto Reference Library, Special Collections Department
Fig. 2.3

Crellin was born in Ulverston, Cumbria, England, in 1837 (fig. 1).[18] The Crellin family originally came from the Isle of Man; building in stone was a family speciality.[19] The single critical event in Crellin's career was his decision to immigrate to Oxford County, Ontario, sometime between 1865 and 1869.[20] An informal family history called "Branches" tells that the Crellin and McComb families were friends in England when the McCombs immigrated to Oxford County in 1850. Crellin married Elizabeth McComb in 1870 and built his first farmhouse for her family. At the time of his marriage, Crellin bought eight acres of land, two kilometres north of Kintore on what is now Highway 119, and began building the picturesque stone house that became the Crellin home.

When Crellin immigrated to Canada, the impact of James Avon Smith's farmhouse designs was already being felt across Southern Ontario. *The Canada Farmer* had been in production for a few years and Canada had just become a nation with Confederation in 1867. The Canadian Bureau of Agriculture was established in 1852 and the farm economy of Southwestern Ontario changed so radically, that by 1867 there were two hundred cheese factories in the province. In 1873, butter factories were introduced as well.[21] In the context of Oxford County, one of the most discernible results of agricultural policies was the change from wheat to dairy farming. As a consequence, farmers were making money and the visual aspect of their farms changed accordingly. Shanties and wood frame buildings were replaced or supplemented by picturesque masonry houses that by their very nature were expensive. In an article written for the November 15, 1872, issue of *The Canada Farmer*, an author visiting Southwestern Ontario farms stated:

Formerly, on my last visit, these men, in very many cases, had "poor conveyances, or none, poor horse teams, and often only oxen, almost always there were old log houses," and old log barns and, with few exceptions, very poor fences. Now the case is most materially altered for the better, and I am pleased to record, that in a vast number of cases these men have good, and even handsome buggies, and occasionally good double seated wagons, drawn by fine horses, with good substantial, and even ornamental harness. These have replaced the old teams and the log barns are gradually ceasing to exist as such, but are degraded into cattle sheds. Good substantial frame barns are now seen in every direction. There are still occasionally seen some old log houses that are inhabited, a memento of former "raisings" and beginning in the bush. But, very often these stand close by good frame or brick edifices, well and comfortably furnished [sic].[22]

Crellin thus immigrated to a rural context transitioning toward more lucrative and stable farm production. It was there that he would make his career building homes for a prosperous clientele. The twelve houses that can be firmly attributed to him are situated in the northwest quadrant of Oxford County on dairy farms scattered through the countryside near Thamesford, Kintore, Medina, Lakeside, Wildwood Park, Embro, and Golspie, all sites located north and west of Woodstock, the county seat.

This article is based on a close analysis of these twelve buildings, which can be dated to the period between 1870 and 1891. One source of inspiration was very likely five drawings published by Smith in *The Canada Farmer*. Each of the designs will be listed in the order published by Smith along with the twelve Crellin farmhouses and the date of each house if known. The first design is the "Suburban Villa or Farm House"[23] that appeared in *The Canada Farmer* in 1864 (fig. 2.1), also known as the "L," "bent," or the "cross wing house.["24] The six houses by Crellin based on this model are: the Duncan house, 1872 (fig. 3); the Crellin house, c. 1878 (fig. 4); the Clarke house, 1882 (fig. 5); the Towle house (a two-story version), c. 1885 (fig. 6); the Lawrence (fig. 7) and the Alexander Sutherland houses, both from 1891 (fig. 8). The second design by Smith that inspired Crellin's clients was a one-and-a-half-story "Cheap Farm House," published in 1864 (fig. 2.2), also widely known as the "Ontario Cottage."[25] The three farmhouses that Crellin built using this model were the McComb house, c. 1870 (fig. 9); the Robert Sutherland (fig. 10) and the McCorquodale (fig. 11) houses, both undated. The third plan used by Crellin is "A Two-Story Farm House" of 1865 (fig. 2.3), characterized by a centre front two-story projection edged in quoins, with a window above the front door.[26] The William Reid house is the one instance of this plan adapted by Crellin, with the date "1885" carved into the façade (fig. 12). The fourth model is the story-and-a-half "Cheap Country House" of 1868 (fig. 2.4).[27] This farmhouse has a centre gable with a wing on either side. The Seaton house inspired by this design has a cartouche in the front gable with the inscription: "Erected in 1873 by Francis German and John Seaton" (fig. 13). The final house plan used by Crellin is Smith's "Design of a Small Farm Dwelling,"[28] a symmetrical house with two equal-sized front gables, published in 1871 and directly inspired by one of Downing's designs (fig. 2.5).[29] The Clifford house completed in 1877 follows this plan (fig. 14). In addition to identifying these farmhouses, my research reveals a complex process by which the craftsman and his clients contributed to transforming those designs into highly distinctive structures

*Duncan House, 29th Line, No. 7006,
near Harrington, Oxford County
Karen E. Armstrong. Fig. 3*

*Crellin House, 19th Line, No. 6150 (Highway 119),
north of Kintore, Oxford County
c. 1903 Carter and Issacs of St. Mary's,
Special thanks to Krista Crellin. Fig. 4*

*Clarke House, 1882,
45th Line, No. 5753, north of Golspie, Oxford County
Special thanks to Steve MacDonald. Fig. 5*

*Towle House, 19th Line, No. 6432 (Highway 119),
Medina, Oxford County
Karen E. Armstrong. Fig. 6*

*Lawrence House, 1891,
209 Allen St., Thamesford, Oxford County
American Agriculturalist, 1894. Fig. 7*

*Alexander Sutherland House, 1891,
Road 74, No. 4358, Golspie, Oxford County
Special thanks to Ken Judge. Fig. 8*

*McComb House, 33rd Line, No. 6603,
near Harrington, Oxford County
Karen E. Armstrong. Fig. 9*

*Reid House, 37th Line, No. 6642 (highway 6),
north of Embro, Oxford County.
Karen E. Armstrong. Fig. 12*

*Robert Sutherland House, Road 74, No. 4357,
Golspie, Oxford County
Karen E. Armstrong. Fig. 10*

*Seaton House, 25th Line, No. 6594,
Lakeside, Oxford County
Karen E. Armstrong. Fig. 13*

*McCorquodale House, 29th Line, No. 6565,
near Harrington, Oxford County
Undated early photograph by Joyce Groves. Fig. 11*

*Clifford House, 31st Line, No. 7144,
Wildwood Park, Oxford County
Karen E. Armstrong. Fig. 14*

that incorporated not only up-to-date planning and technology, but also a sophisticated visual aesthetic derived from the very soil upon which these houses were built.

> **THE STONEMASON'S AESTHETIC: ABERDEEN BOND AND CONSTRUCTED POLYCHROME**
> "Of the many broad divisions under which architecture may be considered, none appear to me more significant than that into buildings whose interest is in their walls..."
> - *Ruskin, The Lamp of Power.*[30]

In all his houses, Crellin used a distinctive pattern of stone construction I will refer to as "Aberdeen Bond." This masonry style began to evolve at the end of the eighteenth century in and around Aberdeen, Scotland. Small stones called "pinnings" or "cherry caulking"[31] were used to fill the gaps between large blocks of granite (fig. 15). In all of Crellin's houses, regularly cut "snecks" (three equal-sized small squared stones) were stacked vertically between larger rectangular blocks (fig. 16).[32] On the front façades of Crellin's houses, each course begins at the corner with a white limestone quoin, followed by three small square snecks of black basalt over pink granite over black basalt stacked to the height of the quoin. The stack of snecks is followed by a single large block of quarry-faced stone, which is followed in turn by the three snecks, and so on across the façade. The larger stones vary in colour, suggesting that each was selected at the moment of construction from piles of stones collected from the farm fields and transported by horses and a stone-boat to the building site. The quarry-faced or "rocky" aesthetic of Crellin's façades speaks of the high level of skill required for their construction, fulfilling Ruskin's contention that it is "a folly, in most cases, to cast away the labour necessary to smooth it; it is wiser to make the design granitic itself and to leave the blocks rudely squared... There is also a magnificence in the natural cleavage of stone..."[33] Contrasting with these rough, fieldstone surfaces, all the quoins, sills, lintels, and voussoirs of Crellin's houses are articulated with white St. Marys limestone. The overall colour palette of each house is thus created by contrasting uniform white lines above and below windows, and along the corners with an infill of subtly varied polychromatic fieldstones. Crellin's Aberdeen Bond farmhouses give the impression of a definite overall pattern that from a distance looks like the weave of a textile or a pattern in tile.

Each of the four façades of most of the Crellin-built farmhouses uses different masonry patterning, indicating a clear hierarchy based on prominence and visibility. In nine cases - Duncan, 1872 (fig. 3), Seaton, 1873 (fig. 13), Clifford, 1877 (fig. 14), Crellin, 1878 (fig. 4), McCorquodale (fig. 11), Clarke, 1882 (fig. 5), Towle, c. 1885 (fig. 6), Lawrence, 1891 (fig. 7), and Alexander Sutherland, 1891 (fig. 8) - a secondary façade is made up of even courses of masonry beginning at each quoin with stacks of two snecks in random colours rather than three (fig. 17). In all these cases, this secondary façade faces a driveway. The wall of the house opposite the driveway side is made up of courses of squared blocks of fieldstone of similar size with no snecks, while the back wall of the kitchen wing is rubble. If the kitchen wing was not built by Crellin, the back of the house is built of rubble as in the case of four houses: McComb, 1870 (fig. 9), Seaton, 1873 (fig. 13), Robert Sutherland (fig. 10), and McCorquodale (fig. 11) (the date of the latter two houses is unknown).

In one instance - the McComb house which was likely Crellin's first - the north secondary façade follows exactly the same patterning as the east front façade with stacks of three snecks between larger blocks, suggesting that Crellin was new to the use of Aberdeen Bond. He arrived at the colour combination of black over pink over black snecks at the second-floor level of both façades of the McComb house after many experiments using coloured snecks in various combinations, on the east and north walls facing the driveway that encircled the house. The south wall of the house on this driveway is made up of courses of quarry-faced blocks alternating with stacks of two randomly coloured snecks, such that three sides of the McComb house are built in Aberdeen Bond, two of which use courses containing three snecks and one with courses of two stacked snecks.

In the two remaining instances of Crellin's work - the Robert Sutherland house (fig. 10) and the Reid house, 1885 (fig. 12) - no special secondary façade is included. The William Reid house has snecks in reverse order - pink over black over pink. In both houses, the two sidewalls perpendicular to the front façade consist of regular courses of large blocks with no snecks. The striking masonry of Crellin's houses seems to be the built realization of Ruskin's dictum that "the smaller the building the more necessary that the masonry be bold and vice versa."[34] We can never know what exactly this extraordinary stonemason was reading, but in these farmhouses we find astonishing parallels between his work and the writings of Ruskin on colour, pattern, and masonry.

Pinnings filling gaps between stone blocks by an anonymous craftsman, 35the Line No. 6432, near Embro, Oxford County
Karen E. Armstrong. Fig. 15

Crellin's Aberdeen Bond style masonry, with 3 snecks, McCorquodale House, 29th Line, No. 6565, near Harrington, Oxford County
Karen E. Armstrong. Fig. 16

Crellin's Aberdeen Bond style masonry with 2 snecks, McComb House, 33rd Line, No. 6603, near Harrington, Oxford County
Karen E. Armstrong. Fig. 17

In Crellin's architecture, Aberdeen Bond was a vehicle for constructed polychrome, a key characteristic of late nineteenth-century architecture in the United Kingdom and North America. Ruskin's assertion that "the true colours of architecture are those of natural stone"[35] is especially relevant when looking at Crellin's houses, as was Ruskin's belief that the best design resulted from "chequered patterns and in general such ornaments as common workmen can execute."[36] William Butterfield [1814-1900][37] in England and Henry Hobson Richardson [1838-1886][38] in the United States were among the many architects who read and were inspired by Ruskin's concepts, the former originating the use of contrasted coloured brick, the latter experimenting with patterns created by combinations of different coloured stones. Butterfield and Richardson were working at the same time as Crellin and their ideas were known through publications, which included photographs of their buildings. All participated in a larger visual culture of architecture that sought ornament and pattern in the qualities of natural materials. In this remarkable instance, Crellin brings to the building site not just competence, skill, and business acumen, but also a true aesthetic sensibility revealed through constructed polychrome. Aberdeen Bond was used by other stonemasons throughout Southern Ontario, but none of those buildings use a regularized colour pattern.

It probably took Crellin and his crew of eight to thirteen men from early spring to late fall to complete the stonemasonry on a farmhouse.[39] Crellin's main income came from building stone barn[40] and house[41] foundations along with stone walls surrounding properties and stone entrance pillars. During the last half of the nineteenth century, the culture of ornament and the desire for sophisticated, distinctive patterning in construction was such that if farmers only had a barn or house foundation built by Crellin, some paid extra to have the Aberdeen Bond style on the side of their buildings that faced the road (fig. 18). Farmers thus signalled to passers-by that they were aware of the latest trends in stone masonry and they could afford the best.

> **FORM FOLLOWS FUNCTION AND FASHION: NEW TECHNOLOGIES, PLANNING, AND MATERIALS**
> "Strong and frank – telling its own story at a glance... it is neither mean nor meagre."
> - Smith, *The Canada Farmer*.[42]

Crellin was a smart businessman whose well-to-do farmer clients were intent on showing they were modern. In their houses, they fused five designs (fig. 2) from *The Canada Farmer* and Crellin's masonry aesthetic with contemporary trends apparent in new buildings in nearby London.[43] Just as Crellin transformed the exterior wall articulation of Smith's house designs, window shapes and roof detailing were updated as well, drawing on such notable examples, perhaps, as the new London Custom House (1870-1873)[44] and the City Hospital (1875)[45] designed by William Robinson [1812-1894] in a restrained Second Empire style. New public and private architecture in other nearby centres such as Ingersoll, St. Marys, Stratford, and Woodstock no doubt also provided inspiration.

*Crellin's Aberdeen Bond barn foundation,
13th Line, No. 6332, Oxford County
Karen E. Armstrong. Fig. 18*

*Alexander Sutherland House, French Doors, 1891,
Road 74, No. 4358, Golspie, Oxford County.
Karen E. Armstrong. Fig. 19*

By 1870, when Crellin began building his first farmhouse, the Gothic Revival detailing apparent in some of Smith's designs had run its course: Crellin never resorted to a pointed Gothic window in any of his houses. Instead, he used rectangular "two over two" windows along with segmental round arch windows until his last two houses in 1891, where he introduced the "one over one" and the flattened segmental arch window. Other trends current in London and elsewhere were the use of colourfully patterned slate roofs[46] and decorative cast-iron cresting.[47] Slate roofs were probably used on all Crellin-built houses and original cast-iron cresting can still be found on the bay window roof of Crellin's own house. Of the Crellin houses that still have their original slate roofs, the Towle House has a Second Empire "floral motif" while the Lawrence and Alexander Sutherland houses have a "fish scale" pattern.[48] The veranda roofs of Crellin's houses varied in shape and materials. Some were flat, some were bell curved; some were likely roofed with tin, others with slate. The Lawrence veranda still retains its original hipped roof with a pink floral slate decoration. The stylistic effects of window and roof design in Crellin-built farm houses were clearly important to his clients and referenced recent urban architecture in the immediate region, itself a reflection of international trends.

In addition to being an expert stonemason, his houses reveal that Crellin was also a skilled and imaginative carpenter. There seems to be nothing Crellin could not make and he made it all without electricity. He was the embodiment of Ruskin's dictum "to those who love architecture, the life and accent of the hand are everything..."[49] He crafted the decorative bargeboards, shutters, door and window frames, staircases, and interior panelling for all his houses. He also made furniture, games, and toys still valued by his descendants, including a built-in china cabinet in the dining room of his own house. In 1884 he joined the King Solomon Masonic Lodge in Thamesford[50] and built a roll-top desk with a glass-fronted bookcase above, topped by a wide moulding featuring the Masonic symbol. Changes in technology meant that Crellin could use mass-produced items such as speciality lumber for interior door and window frames. Other factory-produced items found in Crellin house interiors are plaster ceiling cornices, mouldings, and medallions, which could be purchased through mail-order catalogues.

Crellin and his patrons were concerned that the exterior of their houses express the functional aspects of the interior spaces. Like the masonry patterning built from local stones, this emphasis on functional clarity seems to fulfil a contemporary dictum expressed in Smith's articles that "the house should suggest its own story at a glance..."[51] The kitchen extensions on the back of Crellin houses tell a story of the house as a working system, which included cast-iron cooking stoves, storage, pantries, sculleries, and usually stairs to the cellar and sometimes stairs to bedrooms above.[52] There may have been an indoor kitchen sink and pump, however all evidence of a water supply has been lost. A major feature in Smith's designs, the kitchen extension was built onto the back of the houses. In some instances, existing houses on the property were moved and tacked onto the back of Crellin's new farmhouses, a kind of adaptive-reuse recalling an earlier, less affluent phase of a family's history.

As the kitchen extensions demonstrate, Crellin and his clients were attentive to technology and functional considerations. From Smith's designs to Crellin's houses, the evolution in heating systems is particularly obvious. In all his designs published in *The Canada Farmer*, Smith used fireplaces for heating. The only fireplace built into a Crellin house appears in the dining room of the Lawrence house. Crellin and his clients realized that fireplaces were not adequate during the cold Canadian winters, so before 1882 his houses were heated exclusively with castiron stoves. From the 1882 Clarke house onward, Crellin installed the new "free or hot air" furnaces in his cellars that burned wood or coal and relied on convection to distribute heat throughout the house. Such systems proved inadequate, so Crellin continued to include cast-iron heating stoves along with furnaces in his houses. None of these cast-iron stoves or furnaces remain, but an early interior photograph of the 1891 Lawrence house shows a parlour stove with a smoke pipe attached to the ceiling.[53]

> **BUILDING A MODEL FARM HOUSE: THE LAWRENCE HOUSE (1891)**
> "Every man has, at some time of his life, personal interest in architecture."
> - *Ruskin, The Stones of Venice.*[54]

Detailed research carried out on all the Crellin houses, together with an array of surviving documents, photographs, and owner testimonials, suggest that his clients had a major role in the decision-making process before and during the construction of their farmhouses. Published designs in *The Canada Farmer*, local models, and new products all played a part in their thinking. Space does not permit a detailed account of all Crellin farmhouses; here, I will provide an analysis of the Lawrence house of 1891, which not only stands as the culmination of Crellin's building practice, but also reveals the exceptional role of one client, David Lawrence, in the design of his own house. The plan and elevation of Crellin's exact contemporary Alexander Sutherland house[55] is essentially a mirror copy of the Lawrence house, but the Sutherlands had their own ideas about convenience and planning. In the case of Lawrence, the client's published writings reveal the thought process behind the creation of his farmhouse, which appears to be part of a media-savvy strategy to popularize his design internationally as a model. If James Avon Smith addressed a national public through *The Canada Farmer*, Lawrence succeeded in presenting his house to an even wider, global audience.

Located nineteen kilometres apart, the Lawrence and Sutherland farmhouses can be dated by inscriptions carved on blocks of stone incorporated into each house front. The usual "rocky aesthetic" and Aberdeen Bond with three snecks on the front and two snecks on one side facing a driveway are present. Externally, the Lawrence and Sutherland houses resemble Smith's "Suburban Villa or Farmhouse" published in *The Canada Farmer* in 1864.[56] As early photographs show, the projecting front is widened to incorporate two windows, eliminating the projecting bay in Smith's design. The flattened segmental arch and "one over one" windows made their only appearance on these last two houses. An exterior feature that remains intact is the original slate roof with a fish scale design on the front facing the road. The Lawrence house veranda still retains its original slate hipped roof with a pink floral design. The Sutherland veranda was similar but enclosed in stone sometime in the mid-twentieth century and the section on the driveway side was removed. Both the Sutherland and the Lawrence verandas are "L" shaped (a first for Crellin) to accommodate the front door that is located on the side wall of the projecting front or the short end of the "L." Unlike Smith's 1864 design, where one entered the house into a centre hall, one had two choices from the veranda in the Lawrence house. Either one walked directly into the large dining room that occupies the centre of the main floor, or entered into the staircase hall. In the Sutherland house there was the choice of entry from the veranda into the library or the staircase hall.

Both Lawrence and Sutherland appear to have wanted to express their Scottish origins by incorporating the Cross of St. Andrew (the patron Saint of Scotland) into the decor of their houses. In the Lawrence house, this motif is found at the peak of the bargeboards of the two gables on the front façade facing east and in the bargeboards of the secondary façade facing south. In the Sutherland house, the Cross of St. Andrew appears in ornamental frosted glass windows of three interior French doors (fig. 19). If this glass was created in 1891 at the same moment as the house, the only local art glass manufacturer was R. Lewis in London, who had no competition until the late 1890s when Hobbs Hardware set up a plant to manufacture art glass.[57] In the construction photo of the

Alexander Sutherland House, construction site, 1891, Road 74, No. 4358, Golspie, Oxford County. Special thanks to Ken Judge. Fig. 20

Sutherland house (fig. 20), Lawrence and Sutherland are shown in a moment of Scottish solidarity, each clasping the other's forearm with one hand. Lawrence holds a roll of paper in his right hand and Sutherland appears to be gesturing to both of them with his left hand, saying: "We Scots worked together on the design of my house."

Bathroom technology seems to have had difficulty making in-roads in rural areas.[58] Apparently, Crellin installed no bathrooms before the Lawrence and Sutherland houses. In the five house designs by Smith that appear to have inspired Crellin and his clients, only one incorporated a bathroom.[59] As Lawrence writes in his article, the bathroom located on the ground floor is "supplied from a cistern overhead that is filled from the roof."[60] The water for the laundry is similarly "obtained from a cistern which like that of the bathroom is supplied from the roof."[61] The Lawrence and Sutherland bathrooms are the only definite instances of Crellin incorporating these features into his farmhouses. The appearance of bathrooms in the main floor plan of both the Lawrence and Sutherland houses is a clear sign of innovation, as was the inclusion of built-in closets in four of the five upstairs bedrooms in the Lawrence house. In Smith's 1864 house plan that may have served as Lawrence's model, only one bedroom included a closet.[62]

More striking still, in both the Lawrence and Sutherland houses, is the development of complex, functional cellar arrangements lit by prominent windows and paved with cement floors. Crellin's earlier houses reveal that cellars were dug out and included windows while others were partially excavated with crawlspaces under the kitchen wing. Most had earthen floors while the Seaton house has a partially dug out cellar with a flagstone floor. As Lawrence wrote in 1894, his cellar floor was made of Portland cement (a first for Crellin). In the 1880s, *The American Architect and Building News* featured articles such as "The Adhesive Strength of Portland Cement" and "A New Method for Manufacturing Portland Cement" that Lawrence may have read.[63] By 1893, Portland cement was available from the London firm of George T. Mann, suggesting that Lawrence and Sutherland were early adopters of this new material.[64] Cement floors heralded the beginning of the end of extensions on the back of farmhouses. The Lawrence house cellar is divided into "five connecting compartments"[65] and includes a milk room with a dumb waiter to the pantry above, a furnace room, and storage areas for apples, potatoes, and firewood. It is accessed by two staircases inside the house, one from the kitchen, the other being a continuation of the main staircase at the front of the house leading down to the laundry room, which contained a cement tub fed by a cistern. With these improvements, cellars were becoming a functioning part of the house. Lawrence emphasized this on his house exterior by showing all six, partially above ground cellar windows, each articulated with prominent flattened segmental arches embellished with the same white St. Mary's limestone voussoirs as the windows above. It is clear that in 1891, cellars were becoming more functional and that plumbing was finding its way into new homes in rural Ontario.

AN EXCEPTIONAL FARMER-CLIENT: DAVID LAWRENCE

"Our country is now about to take its place as one of the great Confederations of the earth. Let us show the world that with our rural architecture as well as agricultural progress, we can hold our place on this continent at least."
- Smith, *The Canada Farmer*.[66]

David Lawrence [1849-1915] (fig. 21) was born on a farm near Farnell, County Forfar, Scotland, and upon completion of his schooling spent a year in the office of architect William Fettis in nearby Brechin, 65 kilometres south of Aberdeen. After immigrating to Canada in 1873, Lawrence married Christina McKay and established himself on a farm on the northern edge of Thamesford. Although his principal occupation was farming, Lawrence developed many business, religious, and civic interests, becoming a prominent resident of the

David Lawrence
Special thanks to Lisa Bicum
and the Lawrence Family. *Fig. 21*

Lawrence House construction site, 1891,
205 Allen St., Thamesford, Oxford County. *American Agriculturist, 1894.*
Special thanks to Lisa Bicum and Geoff Ellis. *Fig. 22*

Thamesford area. As the Thamesford correspondent for the *Woodstock Sentinel Review* beginning in 1881, he contributed many (unsigned) articles over the years,[67] including a sequence of five describing conditions in the United Kingdom written in 1893 during one of his several trips back to Scotland.[68]

Most significant for this analysis of Crellin's houses, Lawrence published a detailed description of his own house in the July 1894 issue of the *American Agriculturist* (signed "David Lawrence, Ontario, Canada").[69] As noted above, the article is illustrated with plans of the interior spaces, a section of a self-cleaning cistern, one construction photograph taken at the point when most of the masonry was finished and before the roof structure was started (fig. 22), and one photograph of the completed house (fig. 7). Through Lawrence's writings, we are able to gain not only a sense of his interests and personality, but also a clear understanding of the decision-making process behind the design of his house.

Given his early work experience in Scotland, Lawrence no doubt possessed far more knowledge about architecture than any of Crellin's other clients. In an interview published in the *Woodstock Weekly Sentinel Review* in 1904, Lawrence stated that he had "prepared plans and specifications for quite a number of dwelling houses, the training he received in an architect's office fitting him for such work."[70] In the same interview, he said that in 1875 he was secretary to the building committee of the Presbyterian Church (now lost) in Thamesford, and he "took a very prominent part in the building of that brick church."[71] As the early construction photo of the Sutherland house reveals, we know of at least one house other than his own where Lawrence was involved in the planning process (fig. 20).

Details from Lawrence's life and publications allow us to better understand the potential role of clients in the evolution of rural houses.[72] In his 1894 article, Lawrence wrote how his original frame house (still standing across the road from his Crellin-built house) was adequate when his family was small. Lawrence's farm property had a good collection of field stones, so it was decided to build in stone. First, he "went around to see the greater part of the best houses that he had heard of, in order, if possible, to be able to group as many of the latest improvements and conveniences into one complete whole."[73] Lawrence then "put the house on paper using the drawing materials he had in his desk."[74]

Of all the Crellin farmhouses, the Lawrence and Sutherland houses are the most distinctive in plan. Lawrence published plans of the cellar, first floor, and second floor of his house, which permits us to understand the unusual room arrangement and other major innovations (fig. 23). In both houses, the original main staircases with their winding stairs, carved newel posts, and delicately turned spindles crafted by Crellin still intact, ascend to the second floor bedrooms. These staircase halls are accessed directly from the veranda, thus separating vertical circulation from the main floor of each house. From the dining room, seven doors lead clockwise to the main staircase and the veranda on the east side fac-

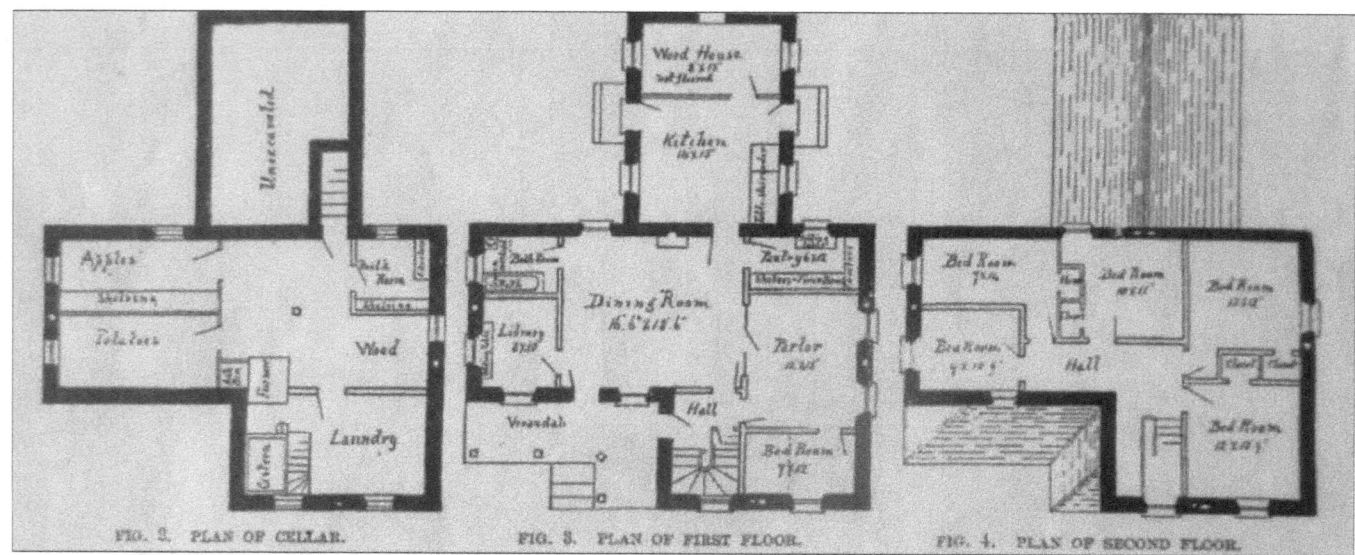

*Lawrence House Plans, American Agriculturist, 1894.
Thanks to Lisa Bisum and Geoff Ellis. Fig. 23*

ing the road; to a library and bathroom on the south side; to the kitchen on the west; and to a pantry and parlour on the north side. Lawrence's concept is close to a "medieval hall" plan and may have been influenced by the Arts and Crafts Movement or currents in American domestic architecture after 1870 that sought to achieve "a new style" or "no style" with new kinds of massing and open planning.[75] Or, Lawrence may have been inspired by the "pair house" brought to Utah by Scandinavian immigrants in the last half of the nineteenth century. It had a single large square room front to back flanked axially by smaller rooms.[76] In my examination of American pattern books and house designs published in the *American Agriculturist*, none includes a plan that could have been an obvious model for the Lawrence house.

As Lawrence continued in his article, a stone house was not cheap, even if the stones were free. He noted: "There are about four hundred and fifty perches of stone work which cost about a dollar a perch; this includes the dressing of corners and arches but not the sills."[77] The slate and slating costs were over two hundred dollars, the carpenter's labour about two hundred dollars, the plumbing, over sixty dollars. Lawrence estimated that "two thousand dollars did not pay for all that had to be paid for…"[78] He also remarked that "there was something like one thousand six hundred meals served to the tradesmen while working at the house."[79] Throughout the building process, Lawrence's wife Christina was probably an exhausted hero in the kitchen. Finally, Lawrence stated that although a stone house is not the cheapest, he believed it to be the best: "it is cool in the summer, warm in the winter, and always dry."[80]

Lawrence was evidently proud of his house, believing he had built the ideal home for his family. His 1894 article for the *American Agriculturist* is testament to his creativity and careful attention to detail in the design of his house.[81] His article stresses practicality, modernity, convenience, and cost, demonstrating how, without a fully qualified architect, a sophisticated, custom-designed and built house could be created and become a pattern-book model for others. Three months after being published in the *American Agriculturist*, the complete article appeared in Australia in *The Sydney Mail* newspaper, a remarkable tribute to the global nature of media circulation in the late nineteenth century.[82]

In addition to mass print media, the railway also linked Ontario farm communities to the world beyond. Not only could farmers like Lawrence travel quickly to urban centres in the region where new buildings, products, and publications could be found to serve as inspiration, but urban travellers from the comfort of railcars could gaze over the rural landscape and glance at the changes wrought by agricultural policies, rising wealth, and aesthetic ideas transported to the countryside through sources like *The Canada Farmer*. As a participant in the shaping of this modern vision of the world, David Lawrence capitalized on the new Canadian Pacific Rail-Line that passed along the northern edge of Thamesford and along the southern edge of his property, which in 1891 linked Toronto to London, Detroit, and beyond. Passengers travelling from Toronto to London were given a perfect view of Lawrence's house, passing within less than thirty metres of the main façade as their train crossed over the Middle Thames River. Clothed in Crellin's striking, colourful, patterned Aberdeen Bond masonry, Lawrence might have regarded his as the most up-to-date farmhouse in Oxford County, if not the province. Canadian rail passengers as well as readers in the United States and Australia were invited to judge for themselves.

CONCLUSION

The foregoing analysis of John Thompson Crellin's stone farmhouses reveal a complex design dynamic in the rapidly changing world of late nineteenth-century rural Ontario. Since these houses can be dated, it is possible to show a significant evolution over a twenty-year period. The houses are the embodiment of Ruskin's ideas about stone walls, pattern, colour, and honouring the craftsman; Crellin was the "zealous and happy workman"[83] that Ruskin admired. James Avon Smith's determination to beautify the countryside by developing *The Canada Farmer* house designs was a driving force for change. The exceptional group of farmer-clients who hired Crellin to build their houses participated in larger, international design trends, benefitted from developments in transportation, mass-production, technological innovation, and used print media to shape their visions of how to live well. The dissemination of texts, drawings, and photographs describing David Lawrence's house to audiences in the United States and Australia underline the linkages between far-flung corners of the globe in which the Southern Ontario farm economy was becoming increasingly integrated.

See Notes on Page 103

Turtle Trouble

The Committee On the Status of Endangered Wildlife In Canada (COSEWIC) has recently uplisted the Spiny Softshell Turtle (Apalone spinifera) from Threatened to Endangered. Reason for Designation Change: The continuing decline of this species in Ontario & Québec is attributed to very low recruitment that has resulted from loss of nesting habitat. Suitable nesting & basking sites have been lost and/or degraded by development, altered water regimes (e.g., dams, floods, erosion of river banks), invasive plants, recreational use & illegal harvest of individuals. Without nest protection, few eggs survive predation by an increased abundance of mammals. Status History: Designated Threatened in April 1991. The status was re-examined and confirmed in May 2012. Again status was re-examined & designated Endangered in April 2016. Scott Gillingwater, Species at Risk Biologist for the Upper Thames River Conservation Authority (UTRCA), said, "We continue to work hard to protect & recover this species, and since our recovery efforts have resulted in proven success in Canada, we can share this model for other sites where this turtle has active populations. As populations continue to decline in most areas, the Thames River has become a stronghold for this species in Canada, due in large part to over 20 years of recovery actions". On June 4, 2016 Scott Gillingwater was the recipient of the W.W.H. Gunn Conservation Award from Ontario Nature. Scott was recognized for demonstrating outstanding personal service & a strong commitment to nature conservation over many years with exceptional results. His lifelong commitment to long-term research on the Spiny Softshell Turtle in the Thames River made Scott very deserving of this award. The UTRCA has been working to recover a number of Species at Risk, including the Spiny Softshell Turtle, through habitat creation/protection, research, monitoring, release of young turtles and education programs.

July 2016 Village Voice

Scott Gillingwater, Species at Risk Biologist for the Upper Thames River Conservation Authority (UTRCA)

W.W.H. GUNN CONSERVATION AWARD

Nominees acting either independently or as a group leader must demonstrate outstanding personal service and a strong commitment to nature conservation over a number of years with exceptional results.

COSEWIC
Committee on the
Status of Endangered
Wildlife in Canada

The Committee on the Status of Endangered Wildlife in Canada (COSEWIC) is an independent committee of wildlife experts and scientists who "identify species at risk" in Canada. It designates the conservation status of wild species.

It was established in 1977 to provide a single, scientifically sound classification of wildlife species at risk of extinction.

The report is influential toward the addition of species to the List of Wildlife Species at Risk by the Minister of the Environment.

Oxford Celebrates Women

By Laura Green

Two hundred people from all parts of Oxford County & beyond attended the 3rd annual "Oxford Celebrates Women" event hosted by Oxford District Women's Institute on May 7. The purpose of the evening was "to inspire women living in the Oxford County area to live a rich & rewarding life and to raise funds for the Oxford District WI Scholarship." The Embro Community Centre banquet hall was transformed with red, black & white décor to fit this year's theme "All that Jazz". The master of ceremonies was Danielle Turvey, 2016 graduate of Wilfrid Laurier University / Bachelor of Music Therapy program & former Embro Fair Ambassador. Enhancing the theme, after dinner music was provided by trumpet players & sisters Laurel Grieve & Sheena Jongerden accompanied by Marlene Matheson playing 4 duets. Productions DJ services from Tillsonburg provided background jazz music to keep the night lively & enjoyable. Award winning actor Seana McKenna, a 25 year veteran with the Stratford Shakespeare Festival gave an insider's look into her life on stage – a storyline that has played out in front of live audiences all across North America! One theme of her presentation was the importance of country – the corn fields & the manure smell in the air. She stressed how "country" played an important role in the development of her family & her husband's family "family tree" & the raising of their son Cal. Before announcing the two 2016 Oxford District Women's Institute (ODWI) Scholarships winners by emcee Danielle Turvey, all former recipients present were recognized with a loud round of applause. The first recipient from 1953 Joan (nee Otto) MacDermid gave the audience a big wave. Kelly Martin, Oxford Centre is a graduate of College Ave Secondary School & will be attending Wilfrid Laurier University in the fall to double major in Music and Math or Music & Science. She has completed 9 years of 4-H Dairy Clubs and has twice represented Oxford County at the Royal Winter Fair with her calf winning All Canadian Calf at one of the showings. After a successful examination in June she will hold an Associate Diploma in Piano from the Royal Conservatory of Music in Toronto. This spring she won the 2016 Rose Bowl at the Woodstock Rotary Music Festival & took home the top award at the Stratford Kiwanis Music Festival. The 2nd recipient is Zorra Township resident Iain Grieve who is completing his grade 12 studies at Northwestern Secondary School in Stratford. He will be attending University of Guelph – Ridgetown Campus in September. Iain has completed a total of 36 4-H projects in the agricultural & life skills areas. He is currently enrolled in 3, including Dairy which is his on-going favourite. Like his sisters, he enjoys music & wrote/played his grade 8 piano exams in April. One of his goals is to become a Holstein Canada Classifier. The evening of fellowship ended with a raffle & a live auction of a pair of Stratford Festival theatre tickets & gift baskets donated by each of the 9 branches in Oxford District.

June 2016 Village Voice

Scholarship Committee Chair Linda Hammond presented Iain Grieve, from Zorra Township with his certificate. Recipient Kelly Martin from Oxford Centre was unable to attend.

Embro

Local Support for Ronald McDonald House

By Laura Green

It was all smiles for 5 year old Carter Innes from Brooksdale when he presented a cheque for $3,810 to the Ronald McDonald House – South Western Ontario on August 5 before he went for his weekly treatment to fight his battle with Leukemia. The money was raised in his honour at the 50th Wedding Anniversary celebrations for Dennis and Carol Turvey – a dear, caring couple on the next road over. Dennis and Carol celebrated their anniversary on July 9 with an open house at Quehl's Restaurant in Tavistock and instead of gifts, family, friends and neighbours donated to the Ronald McDonald House.

October 2016 Village Voice, Embro

Embro Fair 2016

MEET THE NEW EMBRO FAIR AMBASSADOR

By Laura Green

Embro & Zorra Agricultural Society acclaimed 3rd year University of Guelph student Emily Van Bommel from the Thamesford area as their 2016-2017 Embro Fair Ambassador on Fri, Sept 16 at the opening of the 158th Embro Fair at the Embro Community Centre. Emily is taking an Animal Biology Major with a minor in Agriculture. Her future goal is to be accepted into the veterinarian medicine program. She is a familiar face at Happy Hills Resort, Embro for she has worked there for the past 4 years and this year she was Summer Programs Director. She has been involved with 4-H from 2007-2015 with the Embro II and Thamesford Life skills clubs. She has successfully completed 30 projects. Emily also finds time to play Intramural Ice Hockey at the university & works as an Orientation Volunteer at the university. Friday night attendees heard Emily prepared speech on the theme "Farmers Feed Cities" before her crowning. They also were treated to Katelyn MacKay's speech that she presented as one of the 7 finalists at the CNE competition in August.

IT'S FAIR TIME!
September 16 - 18th
Embro Community Centre

FROM FARM TO FORK

FRIDAY NIGHT
7:30 pm
◊ OFFICIAL FAIR OPENING
◊ AMBASSADOR COMPETITION
◊ FAMILY NIGHT SOCIAL
◊ VIDEO COMPETITION
◊ SILENT AUCTION OPENS

SATURDAY
◊ Highland Dance Competition
◊ Road Hockey Tournament
◊ DEMONSTRATION KITCHEN NEW!!
  o Lamb Butchering by Jamie Waldron
  o Cooking Demos
◊ 4-H / Open Dairy Show
◊ Tractor Skills
◊ Monster Truck RIDE NEW!!
◊ Let's Talk Science

COMMODITY ALLEY
OPEN ALL WEEKEND

SUNDAY
◊ Church Service
◊ BRUNCH
◊ Horse Show
◊ Baby Show
◊ Four Paws Flying Show
◊ Pet Show
◊ Silent Auction Closes

MONSTER TRUCK SHOW
SATURDAY NIGHT

TWO SHOWS 5pm & 7pm

PIT PARTY after each show – Meet the driver, take pictures and get an autograph!

BEER TENT: 6pm – 12am

Included with $6 Fair Admission

FREE KIDS ACTIVITIES ALL WEEKEND

ADMISSION: $6 (children 10 and under free) WEEKEND PASS: $12.00
FREE PARKING ON GROUNDS

Embro Fair 2016

Embro Fair 2017

EMBRO FAIR AMBASSADOR

By Laura Green

"Canada Rocks – 150" Embro Fair theme's décor greeted you as soon as you drove past the front lawn of the Embro Community Centre from Sept 15-17, 2017. For there was a huge Canada flag painted on a pile of large square bales (3 bales by 3 bales) in the front yard. Community Service Award winner Eleanor McIntosh officially opened the 159th Embro Fall Fair. Contestants & their sponsors for the 2017-18 Ambassador of the Fair competition were fully introduced by emcee Doug Turvey. Bethan DeRudder sponsored by Jennifer Webb-Century 21 is in her 2nd year of dental hygiene program at St. Clair College. Windsor. Kaitlyn McKay sponsored by the Braemar Women's Institute (W.I.) is in 2nd year Social Service Work – Gerontology program at St. Clair College. Windsor. The judges were Harold Matthews, Kayla Veldman & Dianne Kennedy. While the judges were deliberating, the winning entries for the "Canada Rocks Showcase" video competition were shown & prize money presented: 1st prize Elementary School Age – Bryer Fleming, 1st prize Adult Janice Costa and 1st prize Group Harrington Knox Presbyterian Church. The other entertainment for the evening was "Canadian Face Time Challenge" with Laura Green, John Hazeleger, Lynne Heersink & Kim Topp. Before crowning the new Ambassador of the Fair, Emily Van Bommel delivered her farewell speech. Kaitlyn McKay was crowned the new 2017-18 Ambassador of the Fair. A community social - Only in Canada Treats ended day 1 of the fair.

Embro Fair "Canada Rocks 150"

Sept. 15th-17th 2017

- Game ON Road Hockey Tournament
- Touch-A-Truck
- Four Paws Flying Entertainment
- Let's Talk Science
- FREE Kids' Activities
- "Play All Day" Kids' Inflatables
- Bubble Soccer

www.embrofair.com

Fair Admission
Children 10 & Under FREE • Adult Day Pass - $6 • Adult weekend Pass - $12

Friday Sept. 15th
Exhibits Received 8am-noon
Evening Program
Official Opening of the Fair
Ambassador Competition
Silent Auction Opens
"Canada Rocks Showcase" Video
Competition Presentations

Big Creek Tractor Pullers & Wing Night Karaoke Sept. 16th

Saturday Sept. 16th
Gates Open 8am
Bennington/Cody's 4H Achievement Day
& Open Dairy Show
FREE Kids' Activities
Kids' Inflatables
Touch-A-Truck
Game ON Road Hockey Tournament
Let's Talk Science
Bubble Soccer
SW Ontario Highland Dance Competition
Wing Night & Canadian Idol Karaoke
Big Creek Pullers

Sunday Sept. 17th
Non-denominational Church Service
Brunch
Touch-A-Truck
Heavy Horse & Haflinger Show
Baby Show
FREE Kids' Activities
Kids' Inflatables
Let's Talk Science
Pet Show
Four Paws Flying Entertainment
Silent Auction Closes - 3pm

$10.00 for kids ride all day inflatables.

Bubble Soccer: $5.00 for 10 mins.

Free Freezies for elementary school age children. At the Fair Office.

Community Service Award

By Laura Green

The 2017 recipient of the Community Service Award presented by the Embro & Zorra Agricultural Society / Embro Fair Board has volunteered her time & talents not only to the fair board but to other community organizations. A very surprised Eleanor McIntosh was presented the award at the opening night Feb 25 of the Embro Dinner Theatre production of "Shorthanded" by Michael Grant at the Embro Community Center. Eleanor began her involvement with her community at a young age by helping her mother Mary MacKay with church suppers. In her teens, she joined of South Zorra Junior Farmers whose motto was 'Self Help & Community Betterment". Junior Farmers were always doing something for the community, so joining the Agricultural Society was a natural step for Eleanor. Back in the early 1980's she was the very first female director on the main fair board & later switched to the home craft committee & presently works on flower section. She has sat on many committees within this organization including convening the meal for the dinner theatre. She has the unofficial title as chief scramble egg chef for any brunch prepared by the fair board or Oxford 4-H Association. Besides raising a family of 4 daughters and 1 son, Eleanor McIntosh works along side her husband Bill on their dairy farm north of Embro. She is member of Knox United church, has taught Sunday school and was a 4-H leader. Marian Sterk, President of the Embro & Zorra Agricultural Society made the presentation just prior to the performance & Embro Fair Ambassador Emily Van Bommel assisted her.

April 2017 Village Voice

Little Streetside Library

Embro has joined a worldwide movement to offer free books at a small little "library" in front of Knox United Church on Kincardine St. There are no rules, you can take a book, exchange a book or donate a book. We also have some magazines. And children's books too. All NEW selections as of April 1st! Check it out.

April 2017 Village Voice

Zorra Highland Park Graduation 2016-17

2016

By Laura Green

Traditional bagpipe music filled the Embro Community Centre as Scott Matheson piped the procession of graduates, staff & presenters into the hall filled with proud family members & flashing cameras. Principal Vivienne Bell-McKaig, welcomed graduates & guests to this special evening on June 28, 2016. Anita Fraser representing Zorra Highland Park Parent Council/Home & School Association also gave remarks. Greg Willows, Grade 8 teacher, presented the Recognition Certificates to the following students: Kaitlynn Barber, Hedzer Bergsma, Alexander Bojanowski, Maisie Bracewell, Sara Campbell, Tyler Claxton, Mackenzie Cockle, Tyler Davis, Joshua Dowling, Brandon Fraser, Katelynn Frizelle, Hunter Goodwin, Aria Hart, Mackayla Hayes, Kara Heather, Bradley Markle, Leanne Martin, Jack McIntosh, Sara McNeill, Nicholas Petrus-Froud, Griffin Smith, Haley Stears, Carissa Streatch, Ruby Van Dam, Destiny Walker & Kenneth Wilhelm. Mr. Willows also presented honours certificates. Academic awards: Drama (Thistle Theatre): Mackie Cockle, Jacqueline Witteveen Memorial Art & Music (Witteveen Family) Art: Carissa Streatch and Music: Aria Hart, French (Margaret Lupton): Kaitlynn Barber, English (Brooksdale Women's Institute): Tyler Davis, Mathematics (Don & Sharon Smith): Tyler Davis, Social Studies (Allan & Anne Matheson): Tyler Davis, Health & Physical Education (Elgie Bus Lines Ltd.): Mackayla Hayes, Male Athlete of the Year (Elgie Bus Lines Ltd.): Josh Dowling, Female Athlete of the Year (Elgie Bus Lines Ltd.): Sara Campbell, Science & Technology (Harrington & Area Community Association): Ruby VanDam and Highest Academic (Ann & Dave Parker): Tyler Davis. Other awards: Citizenship (Thistle Lodge No. 250): Hedzer Bergsma, Perseverance (Zorra Caledonian Society):Sara McNeill, Jean Hossack Memorial Award (Ken Minler): Tyler Davis, Katelynn Innes Memorial Award (Margo & Rick Innes): Kaitlynn Barber, Arjen Pelders Memorial Award (Mardine Pelders & Harry Van Egdom, Oxford Farm Safety): Jack McIntosh, Cody Henshaw Memorial Award (Denise Henshaw & David Green, Greenholm Farms): Griffin Smith and Principal's Award (Vivienne Bell-McKaig, Zorra Highland Park PS): Aria Hart. The Dr. Gordon Murray Scholarship by Rosalind Bradford to 3 students – Kaitlynn Barber, Haley Stears & Ruby VanDam. Chosen by their peers, Kaitlynn Barber & Sara Campbell were this years Valedictorians and were presented plaques from Greg Willows & Bob Duplain. Kaitlynn Barber will be attending Ingersoll District C.I. and Sara Campbell will be attending St. Michael Catholic Secondary School, Stratford. Closing Remarks were given by Vivienne Bell-McKaig, Principal. A social time followed the presentations.

September 2016 Village Voice

2017

By Laura Green

2017 will be remembered as Canada's 150th birthday, but for 25 grade 8 students it will be remembered as the year that they finished grade 8 at Zorra Highland Park School (ZHPS) and started a new phase of their education – high school life – new classmates, new teachers & new styles of learning. Graduation celebrations were held June 28, 2017 at the Embro Community Center with the processional led by Piper Scott Matheson. Welcome remarks were given by Vivienne Bell-McKaig, Principal. Remarks were also given by Anita Fraser, ZHPS Home & School Association. Greg Willows & Mark Crockett presented the Recognition Certificates to the following students: Ainsley Alyea, Samantha Borland, Aleisha Brenneman, Destiny Brenneman, Daron De Rudder, Jack Donner, Mick Donker, Samuel Donker, Brodie Doucette, Connor Dow, Khadija Fraser, Owen Fraser, Eric Kramer, Mya MacKay, Rebecca McIntosh, Logan Munro, Kaitlyn Noble, Oliver Robotham, Emily Smith, Eric Stoddart, Caleb Tomen, Abbey Walker, Isaac Westlake, Caleb Whetstone & Nicole Wilhelm. Subject awards winners & sponsors: Drama (Thistle Theatre) Caleb Tomen & Daron De Rudder, English (ZHPS) Mya MacKay, French (Margaret Lupton) Nicole Wilhelm, Mathematics (Sharon Smith) Ainsley Alyea, Health & Physical Education (Elgie Bus Lines) Caleb Whetstone, Social Studies (Al & Anne Matheson) Khadija Fraser, Science & Technology (Harrington & Area Community Association) Eric Kramer, Jacqueline Witteveen Memorial Art (Witteveen Family) Kaitlyn Noble, and Music Aleisha Brenneman & Mick Donker. Female Athlete award (Elgie Bus Lines) Destiny Brenneman and Male Athlete (Elgie Bus Lines) Mick Donker. Citizenship Award (Thistle Lodge No. 250) Caleb Whetstone, Perseverance Award (Zorra Caledonian Society) Khadija Fraser, Oxford Farm Safety in memory of Arden Pelders, Logan Munro, Katelynn Innes Memorial Award (Rick & Margo Innes) Connor Dow; and Cody Henshaw Memorial Award (Greenholm Farms) Owen Fraser. Ainsley Alyea won the Highest Academic (Ann & Dave Parker), the Principal's Award (Vivienne Bell-McKaig) and Jean Hossack Memorial Award. The Dr. Gordon Murray Scholarships (Rosalind Bradford) were awarded to Becky McIntosh, Nicole Wilhelm & Mya MacKay. The Hickson Lion's Club Bursary was awarded to Becky McIntosh. Valedictorians this year were Connor Dow & Mya MacKay.

September 2017 Village Voice

THAMESFORD MILL
1949

Thamesford

Thamesford Trojans

The Trojans are a community owned and organized team with a volunteer board of directors. They are a part of the Ontario Hockey Association ("OHA") and have been incorporated since 1976. They are currently a member of the Ontario Junior "C" Hockey league, in the newly created Southern Ontario Junior Hockey League ("SOJHL"). The SOJHL previously consisted of 15 teams, but after a re-alignment by the OHA in the spring of 2013, the SOJHL was reduced to nine teams, with the exit of all seven teams that remained from the old McConnell conference and the addition of the Aylmer Spitfires.

The Trojans have been a very successful organization with many accomplishments, including the following.

- 39 years of operation
- nine Ontario championships (only team in Jr D history with that many)
- 12 conference championships

- Most notable of these championships were the 1989 - 1992 seasons and the 2010 - 2012 seasons, where the Trojans won the Ontario title for three consecutive seasons, being the only team in the league history to accomplish this feat not only once, but twice.

With a rich history like the Trojans have, they also have many proud alumni, Including Steve Rucchin, who went on to play in the NHL from 1994 - 2007, including being the captain of the Anaheim Mighty Ducks from 2003 - 2005. The Trojans hold an alumni tournament every five years to allow the almost 500 former players a chance to compete against each other and re-live some of their junior hockey moments with old teammates.

The Trojans organization recognizes and respects the educational values of young players who are completing post-secondary programs while playing for the team. This flexibility and understanding allows the players to pursue their educational goals while giving them a place to showcase their hockey talents at a competitive junior level. With the help of the Trojans organization, a number of former players have also gone on to receive scholarships to prestigious schools throughout the US, with the most recent being Mike Pye and Byron Budden heading to Lindenwood University in St. Louis. We are very proud to say that along with championship rings, many of our alumni have earned degrees while with the Trojans in various professional fields including business, accounting, engineering and law and have continued on to enjoy successful careers in their respective fields.

The Trojans' involvement in the community is also worth mentioning. They offer various volunteer positions to local students, allowing them to complete the volunteer requirement for their Ontario Secondary School Diploma. These positions provide valuable experience in such areas as videography, sports broadcasting and sports marketing. Our younger minor hockey players are also included in every home game, giving players the opportunity to impress their family, friends and fans in a shootout competition.

The Trojans players participate in local community events. The local family day activities allow our future hockey stars to interact with current players, who are often role models that the young players look up to. Members of the Trojans have often heard that events like these have helped to build self-confidence and pride in the younger generation, which is critical as they grow through life. The Trojans, feel as an organization, that this is a great way for the team to give back to the community and to the young players who support them throughout the year.

Mark Hominick is a Canadian retired mixed martial artist who competed in the featherweight division for the Ultimate Fighting Championship, the WEC, and Affliction. He is also a former TKO Featherweight Champion. He was well known for his outstanding boxing skills and very technical punching techniques, often utilizing the jab. He was born in Thamesford, Ontario. As a teen he attended Ingersoll District Collegiate Institute.

Kids Program With Mark Hominick

AC/DC (After sChool/Definitely Cool): Westminster United Church, Thamesford's Tuesday program is lead by Mark Hominick. Kids learn life skills, fitness, as well as martial arts. The 4:45-6pm program, still has spots available for Grades 4-8. Visit www.making-connexions.com or contact our Child and Youth Ministers, Joel & Leslie Wallman at 519-320-0199 or lmwallman@gmail.com for more information.

November 2016 Village Voice

MY IMPRESSIONS OF CANADA

Written by Mrs. Alwyn Patience when she came to Canada from Germany after marrying a Canadian soldier in 1947.

The maples with their multi coloured leaves, the warm fall days with their slight smoky smell. Thanksgiving when everyone is sending a silent prayer of thanks to God, the short winter days & the all importance of Christmas when once again the whole family assembles and all the minor arguments are forgotten & forgiven. The snow banks & the excitement when at last, a slow plough digs a narrow pathway. The rush of spring which in no time becomes summer. The pungent smell of freshly mown hay, the presentations of newcomers, full of well-meant jokes. The quilting parties of the Ladies Guild and the missionary meetings Saturday night. Shopping in town, a visit to a movie and the smell of popcorn, so unfamiliar to everyone who is not used to their continent yet. Car rides on Sunday afternoons & huge advertisements whose colours all look the cheaper against the quietly coloured countryside. These, and many others are the impressions I forst gained of Canada. There are the stories of De La Roche, Stephen Leacock, Hugh MacLennan, all typically Canadian, all seeing this vast country with a different eye. The amusement of the party line, the versatile housewives, cooking, cleaning & sewing or giving a talk or programme at the local Women's Institute. This is Canada, its people still aware of those differences originating during the wars long ago, full of pioneer spirit still, yet young in it's conditions and its outlook. Opening new areas, experimenting, expanding, developing mines, eager & yet set in their ways. That is the Canada I have found, a county so full of opportunity for anyone who is willing to stand on his own feet & work. A country where nature still has abundance for everyone and a country that has given me a home. Where peace & quiet reign, away from "isms" and mass cruelty. Canada, a land with an important future, not trying to fit together the pieces out of debris, but making a pattern out of a new land. Rivers, lakes & forests belonging to a people who so often dop not even know how lucky they are to be Canadians.

Village Voice 2016

Santa Claus Parade

Calithumpian Presents the
14th Annual Christmas Parade
December 18, 2016 ~ 6pm

Set up 5:30pm at Arena

Parade starts and ends at the Arena

No pre-registration required

Thamesford Fire Station Open House 2016

The Village Bell

A village bell was on top of the blacksmith shop at the NE corner of Dundas & George Streets. Mr. Dinner faithfully rang the bell at 8am, 12pm, 1pm, and 5pm as a call to start or finish work. It was also used as an alarm signal to assemble residents of the village. The bell rang out to celebrate the end of two World Wars.

The bell was hung in the new Fire Truck Hall on the NW corner of George & Delatre Streets which was built in 1953. It was used as a backup to the siren to alert the volunteer firemen.

The bell was moved to the new Fire Hall on Allen Street but was no longer used as all fire halls came by telephone or pager.

In 2015, District Chief Jim Manzer arranged for the bell to be removed from the Allen Street Fire Station. Jim and Sue Manzer had the bell sand blasted and Jim built a new steel base for it. W.R. Smale Co. in Mossley powder coated the bell free of charge!

This important piece of Thamesford's history is now proudly displayed on the front of the new Thamesford Fire Station on Dundas Street at the west end of the village.

Excerpts from Thamesford History, 1994

Chief John McFarlan and District Chief Jim Manzer

The Thamesford Lions presenting their donation

Mayor Margaret Lupton's Remarks

Joe Wallace and Bill Cairns Former Fire Chiefs, Thamesford Station

L-R: Marion Rutledge; Anne Manning (Chief McFarlan's Mom); and Jean Manzer.

Open House photos by Doris Weir

Thamesford Lions Canada 150 Event

Town Crier Doug Turvey

Lion Jack Broadfoot presents flowers to Gladys Rinn for her 101st birthday!

Mayor Lupton

Ellie Teeple singing O Canada

In 1917 Melvin Jones formed the first Lions Club in Chicago, USA & it is now the worlds largest service club. He saw the need for a non-politico, non-religious & non-racial organization that helps the community & those in need.

Lions 100th Anniversary Parade Float

Calithumpian 2016

Friday, May 20th to Monday, May 23rd

THAMESFORD PUBLIC SCHOOL THUNDERWALK

CHILDREN'S HOSPITAL BBQ

HOME RUN DERBY • CALI BEER TENT

BRUNNY'S SPORTS BAR & GRILL

COMMUNITY YARD SALES

5KM/10KM FUN WALK • BAKE, YARD SALE

LIBRARY BOOK SALE • CHILDREN'S RACES

EARLY YEARS FUN TENT • ROAD HOCKEY

MINOR BALL BBQ • COPE AMUSEMENTS

BEACH VOLLEYBALL • BOCCE BALL

OUTDOOR BEER TENT

COMMUNITY CHURCH SERVICE

TROUT BRUNCH • TOUCH A TRUCK

THAMESFORD FIRE FIGHTERS CAR WASH

LIVE PET SHOW

FIREWORKS DISPLAY

CALITHUMPIAN PARADE

THAMESFORD ART GROUP DISPLAY

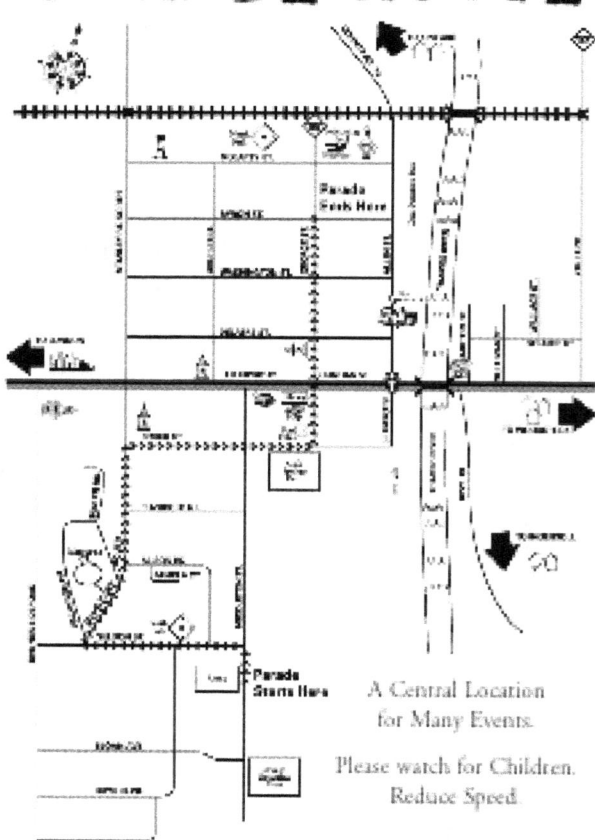

A Central Location for Many Events.

Please watch for Children. Reduce Speed.

Calithumpian 2017

FRIDAY | SATURDAY | SUNDAY | MONDAY
MAY 19-22, 2017

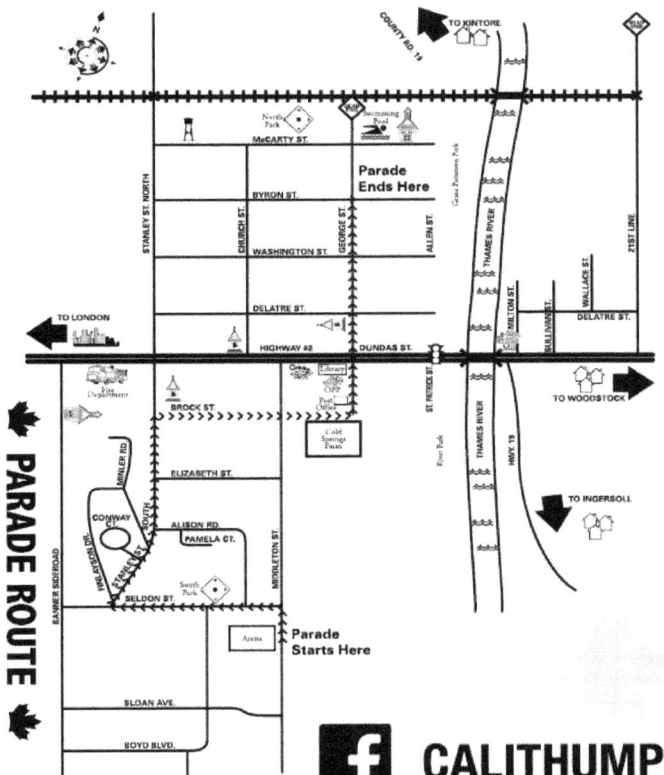

PARADE ROUTE

 CALITHUMPIAN

CELEBRATING THIS LONG WEEKEND

THAMESFORD PUBLIC SCHOOL THUNDERWALK
CHILDREN'S HOSPITAL BBQ
HOME RUN DERBY • CALI BEER TENT
FAMILY MOVIE NIGHT
BRUNNY'S SPORTS BAR AND GRILL
COMMUNITY YARD SALES
5KM/10KM FUN RUN/WALK
BOOKS • BAKE • YARD SALE
THAMESFORD LIBRARY BOOK SALE
CRAFT AND VENDOR SHOW
LITTLE TRACKS PETTING ZOO
CHILDREN'S RACES
ONTARIO EARLY YEARS FUN TENT
ROAD HOCKEY TOURNAMENT
MINOR BALL FUNDRAISING BBQ
BEACH VOLLEYBALL TOURNAMENT
OUTDOOR BEER TENT
FOOD TRUCKS • LAWN GAMES
THE PRACTICALLY HIP' CONCERT
COMMUNITY CHURCH SERVICES
WAYNE PILKEY MEMORIAL CAR SHOW
TROUT BRUNCH
THAMESFORD FIRE FIGHTERS CAR WASH
TOUCH A TRUCK • LIVE PET SHOW
FIREWORKS DISPLAY
CALITHUMPIAN PARADE
THAMESFORD LIONS MAJORETTES BBQ
THAMESFORD ART GROUP DISPLAY
PAW PATROL MEET AND GREET
TPS GRADS FUNDRAISING BBQ
THAMESFORD LIBRARY BOOK SALE

THAMESFORDCALITHUMPIAN.CA

Thamesford Guiding

We wrapped up our Guiding year with a weekend camp for all the groups in June. Brownies & Guides learned some fire and outdoor cooking skills while the Sparks enjoyed a weekend of outdoor adventure. Everyone loved the giant obstacle course at Stevenson Children's Camp. We were lucky to have perfect camping weather & our newest Girl Guides had no difficulty surviving their first camp in tents. We finished off our camping weekend with an advancement ceremony that saw 10 Sparks spread their wings and fly to Brownies, 3 Brownies morphed into Butterflies to fly to Guides & 6 Girl Guides advanced to Pathfinders. All 6 senior Guides completed the entire Guide program & were presented with their Guide Challenge Pin. These 6 outstanding young ladies also earned the Lady Baden Powel award which is the highest award that can be earned as a Girl Guide. All 19 girls who advanced look forward to new adventures in their next level of Guiding. Our group is growing & next fall we will be expanding our program to offer Pathfinders for girls aged 12-15. To continue to provide programming for all ages, we need help. Please contact Heather 519-285-1126 if you are able to help out. Registration for girls of all ages is on-line and you can register anytime, no need to wait for the September back-to-school frenzy. Visit girlguides.ca and select 2nd Thamesford Sparks/Brownies/ Guides/Pathfinder as your unit.

July 2016 Village Voice

Lady Baden Powell Award recipients: Courtney Kittmer, Grace Roddick, Erin Roberts, Jane Sawyer, Georgia Bolton, Claire Sawyer

Jack O'Bright & Wendy Lake draw the winning ticket at the Royal Bank, Thamesford on December 22, 2016

TBA CHRISTMAS ANNUAL RAFFLE BASKET DONORS

Dr. Bob & Joan Houston   Marie Keasey   Tim Horton's
Just 4U Bed and Breakfast   Betty Sloan   JC Graphics
Beth O'Bright   Judy Fickling   Wendy Lake
Pat and Ron Ball   McFarlan Rowlands Insurance
Oxford Mutual Insurance
Pharmasave   Erica Unger Insurance   Tokyo Joe's
McKinnon Custom Framing   RBC Bank
Amanda's Fernlea Flowers
Thamesford Accounting & Financial Services

Thank you TBA! from winner Bev Porter

Water & Wheels
Fund Raising begins

The newly formed Zorra Water & Wheels committee was thrilled to continue plans in January 2017 after receiving budget consideration of $150,000 at the December 2016 council meeting. The building of a Skate Park & Spray Pad in Thamesford is expected to begin in 2018 while ongoing planning & fundraising continues. The committee has been overwhelmed by the support of the Thamesford Lions Club who have selected this project as their main fundraising project with a commitment of $50,000 towards our total project goal of $400,000! Meetings have been held with the selected Ron Koudys Landscape Architects after requesting submissions from local landscape architect firms, a timeline has been formed & site meetings, reviews & drawings have been presented to the committee. Our 1st Open House is planned for Mon, Apr 10, 5-8pm at the Beaty Room at the library. We encourage everyone to attend & provide feedback and consideration for the proposed sites & conceptual designs. The Zorra Water & Wheels committee has been meeting semi-monthly to set community fundraising goals & activities, source grant funding & review drawings & research with RKLA. The committee is excited about the original design logo contest that is underway at our local elementary schools by the students who have prepared delegations for council, canvassed neighbourhoods for support & demonstrated a great deal of enthusiasm for this project over the past year. This process is moving ahead quickly & we will be looking for continued support from our community. Specifically, we are looking for individuals who would like to participate in workshops to discuss the design specifics of what our Skate Park & Spray Pad should look like. If you are interested in providing your feedback or have some knowledge of what makes a great Skate Park or Spray Pad, please submit your interest to waterandwheelsthamesford @outlook.com. Please come out to the Open House & voice your support, suggestions & concerns about the site and scope of our project. Information is available on the Zorra Township website where minutes are posted from Zorra Water & Wheels meetings (www.zorra.on.ca). You can also follow us on Facebook, Water and Wheels Committee.

March 2017 Village Voice

Zorra Water & Wheels was presented with a $10,000 donation from Trillium Mutual Insurance Company and ROOTS (Recognizing Our Opportunity To Support) at the fundraising Paint Night at the Beaty Room, Thamesford Library. Thanks to everyone involved for making this donation possible.
Special thanks to the hardworking folks at McFarlan Rowlands Insurance for seeking out these amazing grant opportunities for this project!

Information courtesy of: Brian Gill
Ower Log Cabin beside the Zorra Township Office on County Road 119.
Both photos are about the same vintage. One shows the cabin as a gas station (above), the other is from when Burt Carr's China Business was the occupant of the Cabin when this road was Highway #2, the main highway across Southern Ontario.

Kintore

Kintore Kids - Easter Sunday circa 1969-70
Back row: Richard McKellar, Lois Woods, Janice Woods, Debra McKellar
Front row: Marcia Woods, Tracey McKellar, Vicki Hammond

Kintore Girl Guides Jacki Hammond, Janet Andrews and Kathy Hogg receive All Round Cord - May 26, 1982

Wedding Picture of Joan Poole & Kenneth Stainton in 1946

Joan Poole was a teacher at S. S. #6, East Nissouri in Kintore at the time of her wedding. Two of her flower girls at the wedding were Jean McKellar, centre who wore a blue dress and Doris McKellar on the right who wore a pink dress. The other flower girl was the groom's niece and her dress was yellow. The ribbons in their hair matched their dresses.

Joan and Ken resided on Highbury Avenue North operating Stainton Pumps and Well Drilling for many years. Ken passed away in 2004 and Joan died in 2015. Both are interred in the Zion 7th Line Cemetery, in West Nissouri Township.

Sunnyside Pond,
Harrington.

HARRINGTON
On Lots 30 & 31 Con 2 W. Zorra
Scale 10 Chs.- 1 inch
RIVER THAMES
CHARLOTTE ST
FRASER ST
S.& Mill
Cheese Factory
Sch
MAIN ST.
P. Office
Grist Mill
PARK ST.
QUEEN ST.
DAVID ST.
VICTORIA ST.
ALBERT
ADELAIDE ST.
CORNELIA ST.
ELIZABETH
M.E. Ch.
WEST ST.
EAST ST.
Ch.

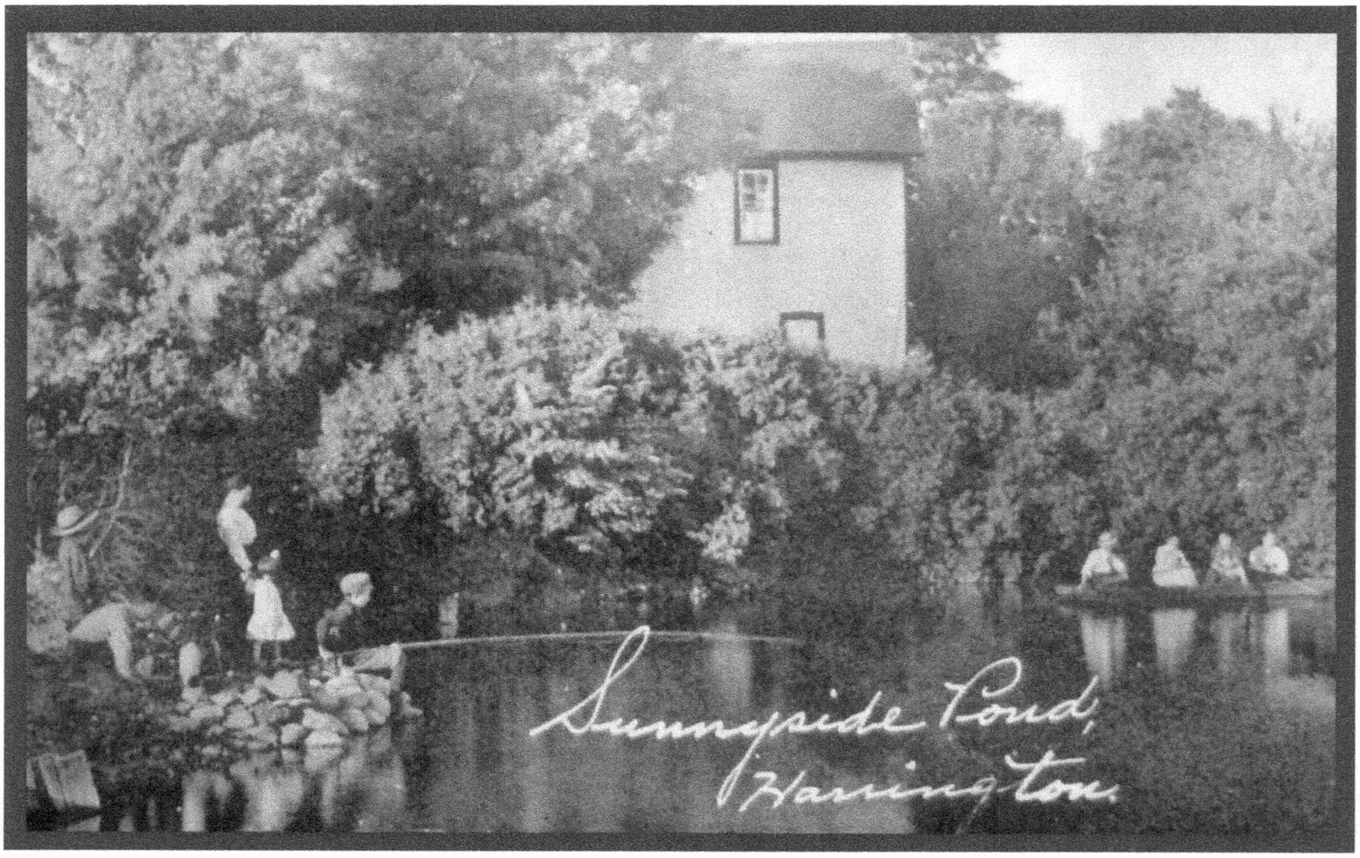

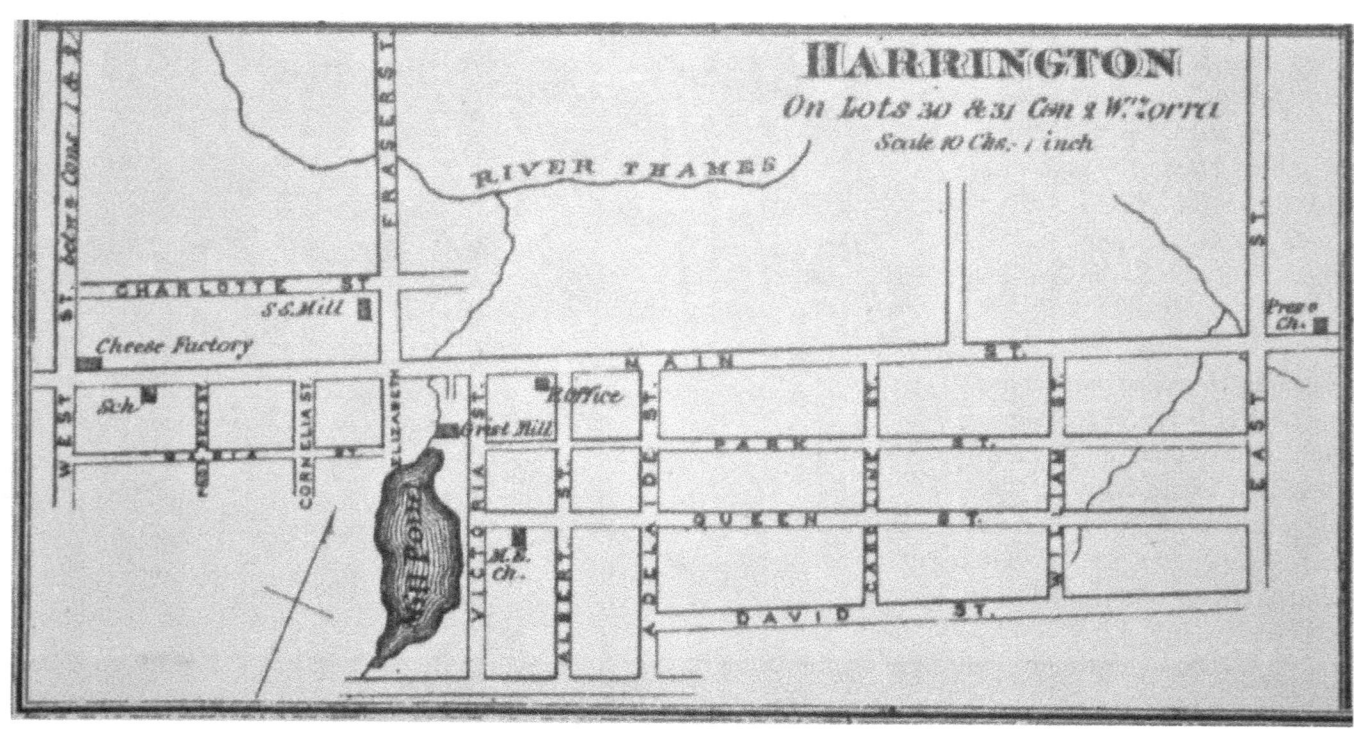

Harrington

150 Heritage Festival

On Sat, Aug 12, 2017 the Harrington & Area Community Association is hosting a celebration of Canada's 150th Birthday! Our goal is to recreate what our beautiful village might have looked like 100-150 years ago. If you have any old photos, artifacts, skills or knowledge that you are willing to share - we would love to hear from you by Apr 30! Email: ourharringtonhome@live.ca or 519-475-4097. The Harrington 150 Heritage Festival is made possible, in part, by an Ontario 150 Celebration Grant from the Ontario Ministry of Tourism, Culture and Sport".

April 2017 Village Voice

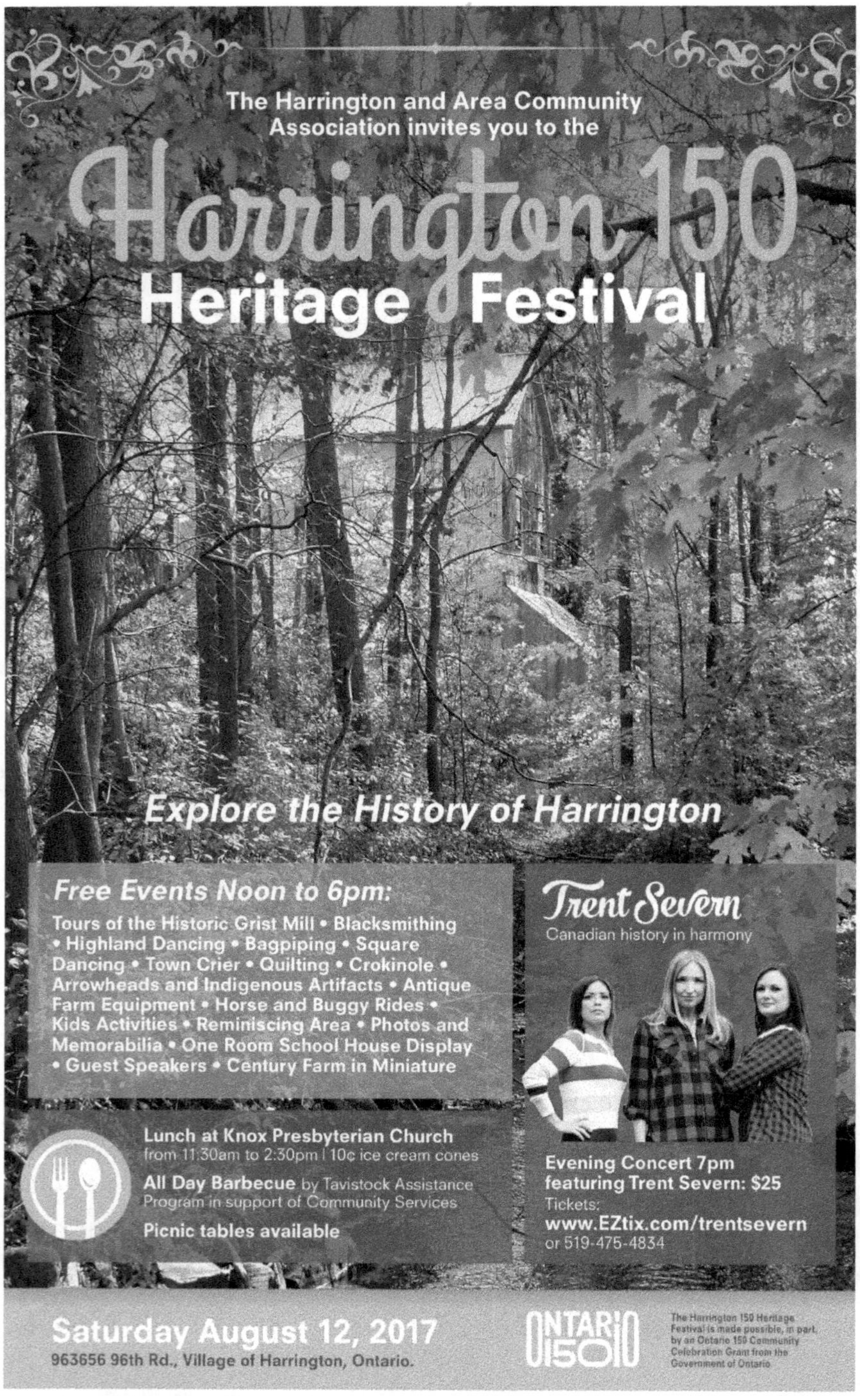
The Harrington and Area Community
Association invites you to the
Harrington 150
Heritage Festival
Explore the History of Harrington
Free Events Noon to 6pm:
Tours of the Historic Grist Mill • Blacksmithing • Highland Dancing • Bagpiping • Square Dancing • Town Crier • Quilting • Crokinole • Arrowheads and Indigenous Artifacts • Antique Farm Equipment • Horse and Buggy Rides • Kids Activities • Reminiscing Area • Photos and Memorabilia • One Room School House Display • Guest Speakers • Century Farm in Miniature
Lunch at Knox Presbyterian Church
from 11:30am to 2:30pm | 10¢ ice cream cones
All Day Barbecue by Tavistock Assistance Program in support of Community Services
Picnic tables available
Trent Severn
Canadian history in harmony
Evening Concert 7pm
featuring Trent Severn: $25
Tickets:
www.EZtix.com/trentsevern
or 519-475-4834
Saturday August 12, 2017
963656 96th Rd., Village of Harrington, Ontario.
ONTARIO 150
The Harrington 150 Heritage Festival is made possible, in part, by an Ontario 150 Community Celebration Grant from the Government of Ontario

HARRINGTON
GRIST MILL
EST. 1846

HARRINGTON
GENERAL STORE

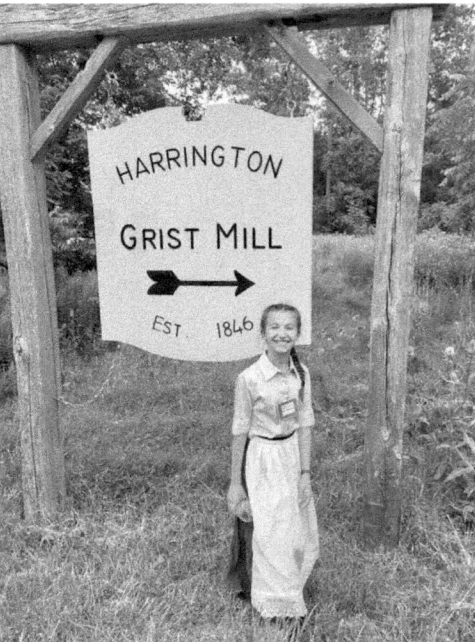

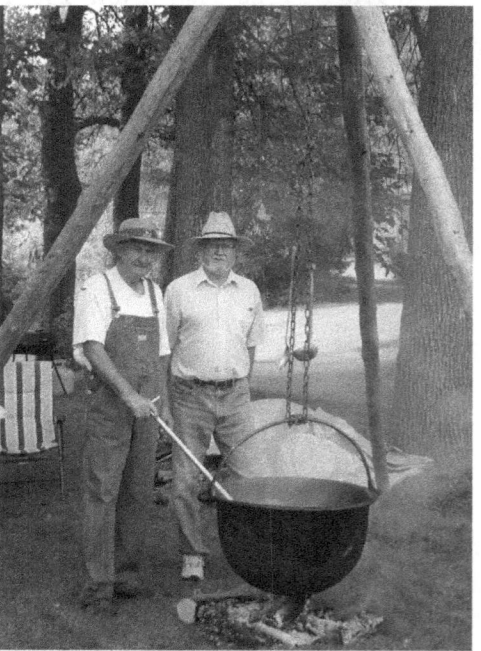

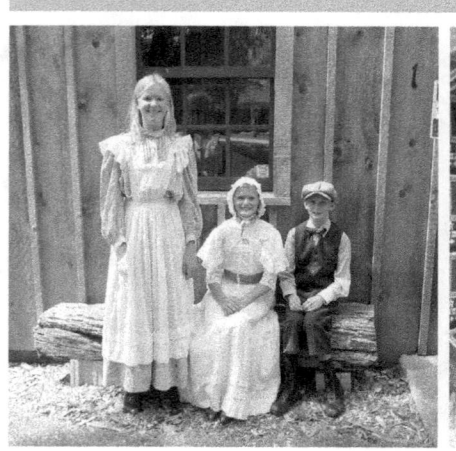

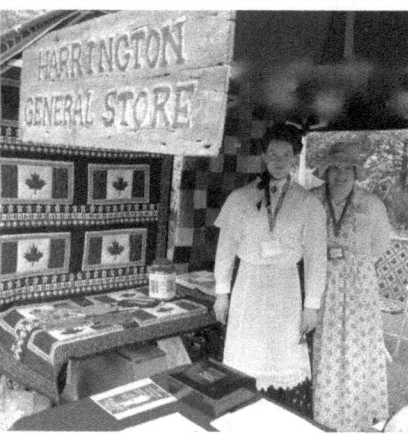

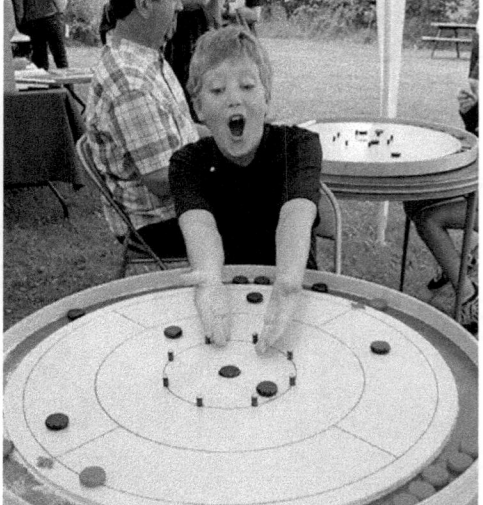

Shown above - the tranquil Harrington Mill Pond - on a beautiful summer day in 2018.

The Mill Pond, source of water power for the Harrington Grist Mill, has existed since 1846.

Please visit our webpage: www.exploreharrington.ca or our Facebook Page: Harrington Community Association for ongoing information about Harrington!

Military

The Battle at Vimy Ridge

The message of Vimy Ridge is one of bravery and sacrifice. The battle, which took place on April 9, 1917, is commonly highlighted as a turning point in Canadian history, where the four Canadian divisions fought together as a unified fighting force for the first time. While 3,598 Canadian soldiers were killed during the battle, the impressive victory over German forces is often cited as the beginning of Canada's evolution from dominion to independent nation. The Vimy Foundation is working to spread the word to Canada's youth — through initiatives like the Vimy Prize and the Vimy Pin — so that all Canadians understand the importance of Vimy to the nation's identity.

To underscore the sacrifices made by Canada, which suffered 60,000 fatalities during the First World War, France granted Canada 107 hectares of land at Vimy to build and maintain a memorial. That iconic site is today considered one of the most stirring of all First World War monuments, and certainly Canada's most important war memorial.

The mission of the Vimy Foundation is to preserve and promote Canada's First World War legacy as symbolized with the victory at Vimy Ridge in April 1917, a milestone where Canada came of age and was then recognized on the world stage.

VICTORIA CROSS

For most conspicuous bravery or some daring or pre-eminent act of valour or self-sacrifice or extreme devotion to duty in the presence of the enemy. The medal was instituted on February 5, 1856 with awards retroactive to 1854. The first award to a Canadian was in February 1857, to Lt. Alexander DUNN (Charge of the Light Brigade). There have been 1,351 Victoria Crosses and 3 Bars awarded worldwide, 94 to Canadians (Canadian-born or serving in the Canadian Army or with a close connection to Canada). In February 1993, Queen Elizabeth II granted approval for the creation of a Canadian Victoria Cross (VC). The Canadian VC maintains the resemblance of the original British VC, except for the insertion of the Latin inscription, "PRO VALORE", replacing the original English inscription, "FOR VALOUR". No Canadian has been awarded the Victoria Cross since the inception of the Canadian version in 1993. Consequently, the following describes the original British Victoria Cross, as has been awarded to all Canadians since the Crimean War.

Victoria Cross information from: THE VIMY FOUNDATION / LA FONDATION VIMY

On The Front Lines of History
Ingersoll Museum

On Sun, June 11, 10-5pm, you are invited to the Ingersoll Cheese & Agricultural Museum to witness & take part in VIMY 100. This immersive interactive public event commemorating the centennial of the Battle of Vimy Ridge is part of the ongoing activities throughout Oxford County to remember Oxford's Own, the 168th Battalion. The entire museum grounds and all of Centennial Park, located at 290 Harris St, will be turned into a World War One site, from the enlistment office and Parade Square, to trench warfare training and the Battle for Hill 290. The museum is thrilled to be working with members of the History Matters Association in order to present this full day of activities & demonstrations. Help prepare comfort boxes to send overseas from the Home Front. Listen to the suffragettes argue their case for giving women the right to vote. Take part in basic training in calisthenics, marching & grenade toss. The Ingersoll Pipe Band will be in attendance to provide music & a steady beat for all those wishing to march. Chat with the Nursing Sisters at the Casualty Clearing Station. Relax in the French tavern. Enjoy the narrated military fashion show including that worn by British, Canadian & Russian troops. Don a uniform & take your picture in the period photo studio before you head to the Front Lines through the maze of trenches. The event, sponsored in part by the Ingersoll Community Foundation, culminates with the Battle for Hill 290. Before you leave, take a moment for a humble & contrite visit to the display on the Commonwealth War Graves Commission and a conversation with a military chaplain. If you have an ancestor who served in the Great War, you will not want to miss this. Come experience life on the Front Lines of history.

May 2017 Village Voice

Heroes of Zorra 2016

By Laura Green

"Hmmm – was that an "ie" or "ei" word and I only have 30 seconds to decide" was on the minds of 17 contestants at the 2nd annual spelling bee sponsored by the "Heroes of Zorra" committee. The event was held Sunday afternoon Nov 13 at the Royal Canadian Legion in Embro. All the contestants were elementary school students living in Zorra Township. All the words used in the contest were taken from the "Heroes of Zorra" website. "This (words from the website) encourages the students to read & learn about our local men & women who volunteered their service to their country" commented Chairperson Shirley McCall – Hanlon. Scott Naisbitt was Bee Master, Margaret Lupton & Roy Youngs - Judges, Time Keeper John Milner, Score Keeper Pauline Hanlon and Sound Man John Hiuser. Winner from Division 1 – Grades 5 & under was Grade 5 student Mackenzie Stears and runner up was Grade 5 student Ava Wilks. Remaining contestants were Nathan Bean, Luke Bloomfield, Tyler Bloomfield, Jack Oliver Innes, Cortney Linton, Matthew Mauthe, Katie Namink, Andrew Power & Jack Woods.

Winner from Division 2 – Grades 6, 7, & 8 was Grade 6 student Arthur Douglas & runner up was Grade 7 student Roserita (Rosie) Verwer. Other contestants were Haley Betzner, Alton Douglas, Katie Schurman and Shannon Woods. Winners from both divisions received Prize money of $100 and runner-up winners received $75. Every contestant received a "Heroes of Zorra" Medal and the experience of testing their knowledge & speaking on stage in front of a room of people.

This year there were 17 elementary school students living in Zorra Township who participated in the "Heroes of Zorra" Spelling Bee contest that was held Nov 13 at the Embro Legion. All the words chosen by committee were taken from the "Heroes of Zorra" website (www.heroesofzorra.ca). Front row: Division 2 runner – up Rosie Verwer, Division 2 winner Arthur Douglas, Division 1 winner Mackenzie Stears and runner –up Ava Wilks. Back row contestants Shannon Woods, Alton Douglas, Katie Schurman, Nathan Bean, Haley Betzner, Andrew Power, Jack Innes, Jack Woods and Matthew Mauthe, Absent for the photo op was Luke Bloomfield, Tyler Bloomfield, Cortney Linton and Katie Namink.

World War I - 1916

Photograph of the 168th Battalion, Canadian Expeditionary Force, marching through Beachville shortly before its departure to England, 1916.

Photograph R2 (Beachville District Museum collection).

Thank you to the Beachville Museum for sharing these photographs from their collection.

Photograph of the 168th Battalion, Canadian Expeditionary Force, marching through Beachville shortly before its departure for England, 1916.

Photograph R4 (Beachville District Museum collection).

Military   93

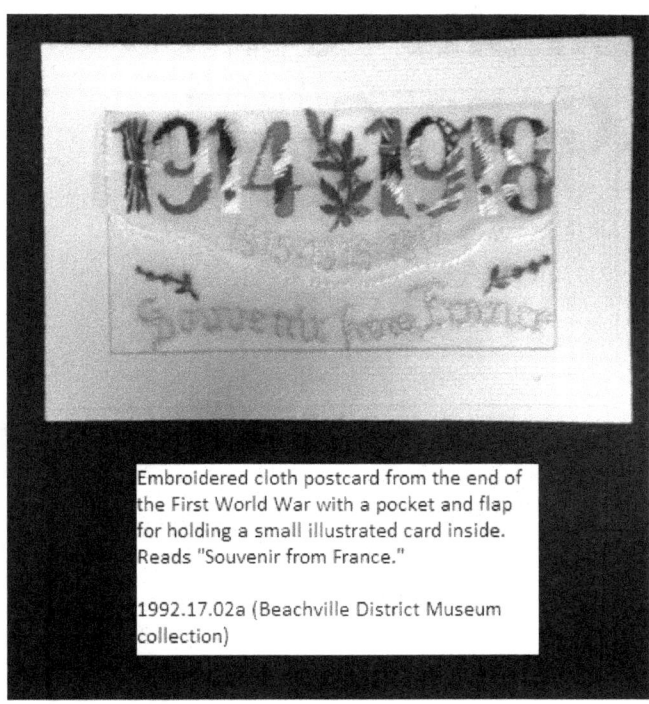

Embroidered cloth postcard from the end of the First World War with a pocket and flap for holding a small illustrated card inside. Reads "Souvenir from France."

1992.17.02a (Beachville District Museum collection)

Embroidered cloth souvenir postcard from the end of the First World War containing images of the flags of the Allied nations that fought in the war. Caption reads "Souvenir of the Great War."

1992.17.03a (Beachville District Museum collection.)

INGERSOLL & DISTRICT HISTORICAL SOCIETY

The Brownsville Historical Society is holding a Remembrance meeting Wed, Nov 9, 1-3pm at the Brownsville Community Centre. There will be light refreshments & the guest speaker will be Marion Honsberger. Please join us as we follow Clarence Honsberger & his brother Alfred on their journey through WWI. The presentation is based on entries from Clarence's WWI diary as well as articles published in the Tillsonburg News. All are welcome. No admission, but donations to the Historical Society would be appreciated. For more information contact Marion 519-642-0246.

November 2016 Village Voice

Ingersoll Museum Musings

Travelling exhibit about Oxford's Own, the 168th Battalion. "Where Honour Leads, We Follow" examines the lives of selected individuals from Oxford who served in the Great War. To supplement that exhibit, the museum will be sponsoring some special seminars on the 21st Battalion (where many of the 168th ended up), the role of the YMCA, and even a special "Donut Day" to recognize the efforts of the Salvation Army during WWI. The big event connected to this special exhibition is taking place on Sun, June 11. VIMY 100 will provide everyone with the opportunities to experience life on the front lines of history. Presented in conjunction with the History Matters Assoc & with financial support from the Ingersoll Community Foundation, the all day military manoeuver will include an enlistment office, a parade square, bayonet & grenade toss training, a French tavern, nursing sisters, a casualty clearing station, a snipers nest & more. You will be able to chat with suffragettes, Belgian refugees, German & Canadian troopers & others. A fashion show will explain what you see & a photo booth will provide you with the chance to get your picture taken before heading off to the front. The day culminates in the Battle of Hill 290 in Centennial Park. If you wish to be a volunteer for the day, contact us at the museum. Many of the activities will be offered again on Mon, June 12 for students in Grades 7 & up. Ingersoll Cheese & Agricultural Museum. 290 Harris St. 519-485-5510, www.ingersoll.ca.977. Winner of 2016 Ontario's Choice Award, Top Small Museum.

March 2017 Village Voice

Dakota KG653 Crash Site Located
C-47 Dakota KG653 Crash

In November of 2017 a researcher in Germany found the site of a Second World War plane crash that killed 20 Canadians. Erik Wieman was researching the Canadian crew of another crash site in his village of Neuleiningen in Rhineland-Palatinate, when he took on his biggest investigation yet -- the Sept. 24, 1944 crash of a C-47 Dakota KG653 aircraft carrying 23 passengers. All were killed. It was among 15 Dakotas en route from England to Italy and ultimately to India to deliver troops building two new squadrons to help in the fight against Japan. One of those killed in this crash was James Ernest Allen of the former East Nissouri area.

Mr Wieman discovered plane parts matching the Dakota as well as a 1920 penny and RCAF buttons.
(Image: Aviation Visuals / Alamy Stock)

The aircraft's journey was plagued by bad weather and navigational issues, which pushed it off course over Germany where it was shot down from the ground in broad daylight. Bullets hit the wing of the plane, which broke off as the aircraft plummeted towards the ground. The gunman, a fighter pilot named Julius Meimberg, later wrote that he only intended to ground the plane.

Erik Wieman considers it a personal mission to locate downed wartime planes, spending hours combing through records and databases. He has co-founded a crash site research group and works to find the relatives of crash victims and memorialize the locations of their deaths. Wieman, a Dutch native whose grandfather fought the Nazis but who married a German woman and moved to Germany in 1992, worked with a local newspaper to find witnesses to the crash. He was shocked when 15 people, all in their 80s and 90s, came forward and offered to help. Decades after the crash, searchers combing an open field last November were able to find pieces of plastic windows, tire fragments and small pieces of aluminum – some still with camouflage paint.

In March of 2018 Colleen Carmichael (a Canadian who was assisting Mr. Wieman in his search for family members of the victims of this crash) contacted the Heroes of Zorra web site requesting our assistance as she had found the HOZ site and noted that there was a James Ernest Allen on the site along with his father and brother. After contacting two of my HOZ colleagues, Joyce Day and John Milner, and determining that they had no further information on Mr. Allen, I thought of my friend Ruth Rout and contacted her. Ruth remembered the Allen family. Not only did she remember them, but that they also had a sister. Ruth was able to give me the name of a niece of Mr. Allen's, and that she currently resides in St. Marys. I contacted her and yes, it is the right family. As well she was able to give me the name of another niece who now lives in the Toronto area. It was wonderful to speak with these two ladies... to hear their excitement about this discovery, and hopefully for them to learn a little bit more about this relative that they only heard their parents speak about. Mr. Wieman and his team have been in touch with the two women. A dedication service of a memorial to these servicemen is planned for 2020.

James was the son of Ernest John and Marion (nee Baldwin) Allen. He enlisted in the Royal Canadian Air Force at the age of 18 in 1941 and went overseas in 1943. His parents had lived at Lot 31 Concession 13 of the former East Nissouri Township and he had worked for Thomas Leadman of Browns Corners. When he enlisted he stated he was a painter.

Contributed by Shirley McCall-Hanlon
Heroes of Zorra Committee Chairperson

Schools

Kintore School S.S. No. 6 1948

Back row: Teacher Grant Gilbert, George Quinn, Audrey Wilkie, Marion Calder, Jean Steele,
Pat Alderson, Barbara Bent, Jim Borland
Middle row: Ron Whetstone, Doris Steele, Ron Hepworth, Ed Borland, Rosemary Whetstone, Ellen Bent
Front row: Elaine Calder, Jean McKellar, Doris McKellar, Dave Hepworth, Jim McArthur, Don Robson, Don Bent

West Zorra S.S. No. 1

1934 Mr. Harvey Kittmer (teacher).
Back Row: Easther Tackaberry, Myrtle Fleming, Catherine Sutherland, Jean Mattson, Florence Mattson, Laura Jones.
Middle Row: Betty Scally, Kathleen Scally, Mary Fleming, Mary Scally, Marion Handley, Helen Hammond.
Front Row: Donald Mattson, Frank Handley, Howard Tullett, Carl Sutherland, Leo Jones, Johnny Murray.

1874 Walker's School

WALKER'S SCHOOL

S.S. No. 1 WEST ZORRA

1869 – 1966

Cover of the book given to attendees of the closing in 1966. *By Nethercott Printing.*
The school was built on 3/4 of an acre of the east half of Lot 5, Concession 1

S.S. No. 3 School Fair 1919

S.S. #3 School Fair, North Oxford, 1919
Beachville District Museum Collection, G-18a.

Agriculture
Oxford 4-H Awards Night

By Laura Green

Party hats for the 100th anniversary of 4-H made their final appearance on the tables of the Awards Night for Oxford 4-H Association at the Embro Community Centre on Nov 20. Lots of well tested 4-H recipes appeared on the table for the pot luck supper. The event was chaired by Chairperson Mel Bergsma who opened the evening with the 4-H pledge which was followed by the 4-H Grace. Guest speaker was Andrew Campbell, a dairy farmer from Middlesex County, a former 4-H member & retired radio broadcaster who spoke on his recent experiences using one form of social media: Twitter – to inform his followers about what life is like every day on his dairy farm. He posts a new photo everyday & started this on Jan 1, 2015 with a new born calf. He stressed the importance of us (those involved in agriculture) to know & understand our consumers. Club members donated items for the FCC Drive Away Hungry campaign. George Klosler, Woodstock's FCC commented on the beginnings of the drive which started 11 years ago. He presented the 100th anniversary 4-H club with a pizza gift card for donating the most items that evening. Klosler will delivery the 409 items to the Woodstock Salvation Army Food Bank. Mayor of Zorra, Margaret Lupton brought greetings from the township & County of Oxford. As a past member of 4-H, she realizes the value of the program & the leadership skills gained. President of Ontario 4-H Council Tammy Oswick-Kearney presented volunteers with years of service awards as follows: New Volunteers in Oxford Julie Schwartzentruber & Carolyn Wilson, 5 year pin; Megan Davis, 10 year pin; Gijs Arts & Julie McIntosh, 20 year recognition; Karen Witmer, 25 year recognition; Marian Sterk and 30 year recognition Geoff Innes. Gay Lea 24 Project Achievement Gay Lea Foods Cooperative Ltd delegate Steven Veldman from Embro congratulated the 2015 recipients from Oxford: Tom Jackson, Trent Jones & Ashley Skillings. Oxford County 30 Project Completion Chairperson Mel presented the to Julie DeBruyn & Emily Van Bommel. Oxford County 60 Project Completion Janneke Van Den Nieuwelaar received this award. Janet Wilson Memorial Award Shawn Wilson presented awards to the Outstanding Novice member Erin Shrigley & Keeton Jones. Outstanding Junior member Laura Witmer & Brayden Gras. Outstanding Intermediate Jessie Carberry & Lucas Swartzentruber Ontario Plowmen's Assoc. Award Eric Howard presented the award (Agricultural Senior 4-H Member) to Tanner Jones. Your Neighbourhood Credit Union Outstanding Overall 4-H Member was awarded to Elizabeth Bruce. Norman Dickout Memorial Judging Awards Bernice & Russell Dickout presented their son's award to winners Novice-Olivia Romkes, Junior-Lilli Smith, Intermediate-Iain Grieve, Senior-Josh Karn and Overall-Josh Karn. Oxford Project of the Year went to Hickson Cookie 4-H Club. In 2015, Oxford had 230 members involved in 15 clubs. There were 53 new members who learned that 4-H is fun & have begun their leadership development. Three members who graduated from 4-H were Paul Knoops, Stephanie Koot & Janneke Van Den Nieuwelaar. The provincial awards of 1st year member plaques, year bars and projects seals were presented to each club."

East Nissouri 4-H Dairy Club

East Nissouri 4H Dairy Club has started up our 2016 season! Our first meeting was held on Feb 20 at Roesbett Farms, home to Gerry & Debbie Roefs. It was great to see our returning members and see some new faces joining our club too! If you are between 9-21 years of age as of Jan 1/16, you are interested in agriculture, dairy, or 4H, you can still join our club. It's a great way to meet new people, learn new skills, and have fun doing it. We welcome anyone to come out and see what it's all about! Please feel free to contact any of our leaders: Nicole Barnett, Racheal Kettlewell, Katelyn Fraser and Christine Baigent. Nicole 519-533-2208, Racheal 519-320-8725.

Village Voice, 2016

Mr. Thomas Ingersoll Visits Oxford 4-H

By Laura Green

Dressed in period costume, story teller Nick Wells portrayed Mr. Thomas Ingersoll first as a young man growing up in during the witch hunts in Salem, the wars like the plains of Abraham, the Boston Tea Party and his migration to Upper Canada with 40 families to his land grant of 66,000 acres in Oxford County from Governor John Graves Simcoe. He named the new settlement Oxford-on-the-Thames and later his son Charles renamed it Ingersoll in his honour. His story telling techniques included role playing with volunteers from the audience. Poor Jane Danen, the chairman's wife had to portray a witch on trail. He also brought with him, a collection of medical instruments like a tooth puller used during this time period. The awards night was held at the Thamesford Community Centre Nov 17 & a delicious pot luck supper preceded the awards. Host clubs were the Thamesford 4-H Life Skills & the Tavistock 4-H Dairy Calf. Jack Danen chaired this portion & welcomed the special guests, 4-H members, volunteers & parents. Awards presentation was chaired by Oxford 4-H Association Chairperson Dwight Hargreaves. New to Oxford this year was the provincial 4-H Cloverbud program opened for youth 6-8 years. Members Megan Ball, Magalie Bray, Braydon Cartmale, Tommy Hampson, Charles Knapp, Fiona Kouwenberg, Meryl Kouwenberg, Tibitha Krakar, Jack McKinlay, Matthew Paulsen, Courtney Pletsch, Lachlann Rember, Jill Strik & Conner Tree received their 1st year Cloverbud membership award. Steve Veldman, delegate from Gay Lea Foods Cooperative Ltd presented the 24 project Achievement Award – a commissioned print which they sponsor to Robbie Jackson, and Shae-Lynn Preiss. Kimberly Bickell will receive hers at her club's achievement night. At the Nov 10 event with The Honourable Elizabeth Dowdeswell, Lieutenant Governor of Ontario, the following members received their print – Megan Couwenberg, Sarah Danen, Brittanie Fraser, Amy Gras, Scott Hanlon, Erin Shrigley & Amanda Witmer. Volunteer Recognition was presented by Mardine Pelders & Judy Hall to: 1st year Christy Brekelmans, Elizabeth Bruce, Karen Karn, Michael Lupton & Hailee Verhoeven, 5 years Racheal Kettlewell, 15 years Vera Van Den Nieuwelaar, 20 years Jim Grieve & Janice Thomson, 25 years Nancy Hargreaves, and 35 years Linda Humphrey. The Oxford 4-H Volunteer Tribute Award for 2017 recipient was Katherine Grieve. Katherine is the current secretary for the association, a 4-H Volunteer, director of the Embro & Zorra Agriculture Society, was a member of the renovations committee for the Embro Community Centre, member of the Zorra Recreation Committee, member of the Brooksdale Women's Institute, Zorra Caledonian Society & others organizations that her family members were involved in like Guiding. As you read, Katherine volunteers her time for 4-H, her community & her family. Presentation of the award will be held at a later date. Provincial 4-H member's awards will be distributed by the individual clubs which includes new member's plaques & project complication seals for 1, 6, 12, etc. Oxford County Project awards: 30 projects Brayden Gras, Devin Gras and Laura Witmer, 42 Projects Julie DeBruyn, Iain Grieve, John Harrigan, and Tanner Jones. Oxford Project of the Year Award was presented to Hickson 4-H Club with their project titled "Let's get ready for the fair". Norman Dickout Memorial Judging Awards for 2017 were presented by Norman's parents Russell & Bernice Dickout. Winners were Novice – Brayden Tree, Junior Amanda Witmer, Intermediate Alex McKay, Senior Iain Grieve and overall winner was Alex McKay. The Janet Wilson Outstanding 4-H member Awards were presented by two of children – Melinda and Shawn. Winners were Novice Female – Kelly DeBruyn, Novice Male Keenan Grieve, Junior Female – Amanda Witmer, Junior Male Jacob Bergsma, Intermediate Female Sarah Danen and Intermediate Male Scott Hanlon. Steve McGregor from Your Neighbourhood Credit Union presented the Outstanding Overall Senior 4-H member Award to Iain Grieve. Sarah Learn represented from Oxford Plowmen's Association presented the Ontario Plowmen's Association Award for Outstanding Agricultural 4-H member to Jessica Carberry. The next event for Oxford 4-H will be the AGM on Jan 31 at OMAFRA in Woodstock.

The Honourable Elizabeth Dowdeswell, Lieutenant Governor of Ontario has personal involvement in the 4-H program! She was a member during her high school years in rural Saskatchewan and as an university student in the Bachelor of Science / Home Economic program at the University of Saskatchewan.

Oxford County Junior Farmers

February 2016
Oxford County Junior Farmers were very excited to celebrate their 101st Annual Banquet at the Embro Legion Jan 9. At this event, we recognized our accomplishments of the past year and presented several awards to members of our club that have made significant contributions throughout the past year or their careers as Junior Farmers. This past year marks both 100 years of Oxford County Junior Farmers and 10 years of the Embro Truck & Tractor Pull. In celebration of these milestones, we are planning a trip to Louisville, Kentucky this February to see the National Farm Machinery Show and the famous tractor pull.

November 2016
The Oxford County Junior Farmers have kept fairly busy throughout the past several months. We had another successful tractor pull from July 29-30 with 6,400 attendees. The pull was a result of the work of many members & volunteers. On August 15 we ran the pre-show for the RCMP Musical Ride in Tavistock. At the beginning of September we had a car rally where members split into teams to complete different tasks around the county to score the most points. On Sept 17, the Junior Farmers organized a tractor skills competition for the Embro Fair. On Halloween we collected food for the local foodbank at our Trick-or-Canning drive in Innerkip. Other plans for the upcoming months include having a float in several local Christmas parades & participating in provincial Junior Farmer events. Through our provincial organization, we are still selling Century Farm Signs to farms in the county that have been within the same family for 100 or more years. We are always looking for new members. If you are between the ages of 15-30 and are interested in meeting youth from across the county while volunteering and helping in our community, come & check us out! We meet every 2nd Friday of the month at 8pm in the OMAFRA building in Woodstock. You do not have to be from a farm to join.

Oxford Jr Farmers Donate $5,000

Oxford-Elgin Child & Youth Centre, the lead agency for child & youth mental health in Oxford County & Oxford Community Child Care, the lead agency for Ontario Early Years Centres, have teamed up to raise funds to support the services they offer families in our community. Together, these 2 non-profit agencies provide free programs that promote healthy development & well-being for children, youth & their families from birth to age 18. Unfortunately, the costs to provide these services often exceed government funding and the quality & quantity of services that they are able to offer suffer. Fortunately, our community has stepped-up to help out. The Oxford Junior Farmers have generously donated $5,000 to Oxford-Elgin Child & Youth and Oxford Community Child Care! The donation will be used to support transportation services for families to & from their therapeutic appointments, clinics & programs.

January 2017
Oxford County Junior Farmers were very excited to celebrate their 101st Annual Banquet at the Embro Legion on Jan 9. At this event, we recognized our accomplishments of the past year and presented several awards to members of our club that have made significant contributions throughout the past year or their careers as Junior Farmers.

May 2017
Oxford County Junior Farmers is excited to announce a donation of $2,500 towards the Habitat for Humanity – Heartland Ontario. The money will be used to help build a new home for a family in need within Oxford County. Chris Budd, president of Oxford Junior Farmers, says "Our club sees the value that HOH provides in the Oxford community, so we wanted to do our part in contributing towards their organization." Oxford Junior Farmers is an affiliated club with the Junior Farmers' Association of Ontario. The clubs work to build future rural leaders through self-help & community involvement. Junior Farmers is open to youth aged 15-29 from rural & urban backgrounds with an interest in building leadership skills & community involvement. Oxford JF is involved with several projects throughout the year, including food booths, the distribution of the Real Dirt on Farming magazine, and the Embro Truck and Tractor Pull. For more information please contact: Virginia, Secretary & Media Coordinator, Oxford Jr Farmers, 519-608-3095, dibblevirginia@gmail.com.

Oxford Junior Farmers donates $2500 to Habitat for Humanity
Back row: Dave Wall (HFH), Drew DeBruyn (OJF), Ben Bruce (OJF). Front row: Brian Elliot (HFH), Elizabeth Bruce (OJF), Janet Bruce (OJF), Chris Budd (OJF), John Harrigan (OJF)

West Oxford Plowmen History

June 2016

The West Oxford Plowmens was organized by 3 members of Sweaburg Methodist Church Sunday school in 1922, Frank G. Murdoch, Stanley E. Allin, and James H. Bastedo, Sunday School Superintendent & Reeve of West Oxford. It followed the successful provincial International Plowing Match held at the epileptic farm north of Woodstock Oct 19-21, 1921. The week before the 1921 IPM plans for an Oxford Association were under review by Warden Johnston, Dr. Atkinson of Embro, and agriculture representative G. R. Green in his office (Sentinel Review Oct 11,1921, page 3 Col 5). J. Lockie Wilson, secretary of the Provincial Plowmens Association & superintendent of affairs under the Dept. of Agriculture was present to open the first event held at Lot 3 Conc 3 farm of Stanton Lick West Oxford on Oct 24,1922. W.O. Grenzebach of East Zorra, who last year (1921) held the Ontario championship for the best plower of stubble in the province won the highest honours in 4 events - first in stubble & sod, best crown in stubble & sod. The 2nd W. Oxford match was held on the farm of Stanley E. Allin one mile north & 1/2 mile east of Foldens, Lot 10 Conc 3 W. Oxford on Oct 24,1923. Contestants in 11 classes competed for $300 in prize money generously donated by Woodstock & Ingersoll merchants. It was a 2 day event, stubble the 1st day, sod on the 2nd. W.C. Barrie of Galt & James McLean of Richmond Hill were the judges. The 3rd annual W. Oxford match was held on the farm of John Thornton Lot 10 Conc 2 Oct 28, 1924. Jas. McLean was again the judge. Lockie Wilson was the principal speaker at the banquet held in Sweaburg Methodist Church basement & Grenzebach was the most pronounced prize taker. J.R. Hargreaves won all the awards open to West Oxford residents. In 1925, the IPM was held at Brockville Oct 13-16. It became a 4 event in 1924 & still is to this day. Grenzebach won the championship of Ontario in both stubble and sod. Petit Gray of Beachville was 2nd in the class for boys under 18 - his first attempt at IPM plowing, a testament to the training & experience he received from the Sweaburg young mens Sunday school class & bringing honour to his community. The 4th annual West Oxford match was held Nov 4-5, 1925, at the farm of Mrs. Warren Cody Lot 5 Conc 3 near Sweaburg. J.R. Hargreaves won the silver cup for stubble plowing open to West Oxford residents only for the 2nd year in a row. Grenzebach was not there on Nov 4. He was at the Perth County match & won the sweepstakes. On Nov 5 he won the open sod class at W. Oxford. The 5th annual W. Oxford was held on Oct 27-28, 1926, on the Hyslop farm one mile south of Ingersoll, Lot 20 Conc. 2. Its rich soil has a pronounced slope to the west. An oldtimer said that plowing matches were held on this same farm 60 years previously. Sod plowing was held on the J.C. Harris farm next Lot 19 Conc 2. One more W. Oxford match was held on the Verne Meek farm south of Ingersoll Lot 18 Conc. 1 before it folded.

Oxford Women for the Support of Agriculture

The Oxford Women for the Support of Agriculture present their annual winter workshop: Peace of Mind - Mental Wellness for Women. Wed, Feb 10, 9am-3pm at Emmanuel Reform Church, 170 Clarke St N, Woodstock. Guest speakers are Gerda Schryver & Katherine Studiman & they will discuss how to strike a balance between our social, physical, spiritual, economic & mental wellbeing, so we can experience optimal mental health. Mental illness and the journey to mental wellbeing will also be discussed. The afternoon activities will include 4 body & mind activities that will have a positive impact on women's wellness. Lunch is provided, cost is $30 for members & $35 for non-members. Day care is provided. Contact Maria Donkers at 519-349-2502 to register.

NOTES:
THE LATE NINETEENTH-CENTURY STONE FARM-HOUSES OF JOHN THOMPSON CRELLIN Pages 44-57

1. I would like to thank my son Christopher Drew Armstrong, Associate Professor of History of Art and Architecture at the University of Pittsburgh, for reviewing and providing comments on this article. I would also like to thank the homeowners of all of the Crellin houses for opening their homes to me and for providing answers. (There are 13 homeowners listed because one of the houses was sold during the time I was researching the article. One owner gave me information on the house and the second owner gave me access to the house). Joan and John Alderman; Lisa Bicum and Geoff Ellis; Robyn and Gary Boulton; Shannon and David Green; Katherine and James Grieve; Jane and Donald Guthrie; Ken Judge; Kathryn and Steve MacDonald; Ulrike and Carl Pelkmans; Doris Seaton; Dianne and Douglas Towle; Amy and Jordan Van De Kemp; Dianne and James Wheler. I would like to express my gratitude to the Crellin family, especially Alice Crellin Ingle, Suzanne Crellin Taylor, Krista Crellin, and Glen Crellin. Many thanks to Hugh McVittie and John Alexander Lawrence, grandsons of David Lawrence, for photographs and information on David. My thanks to Professor Emeritus of Geology Gerard V. Middleton at McMaster University for giving me an on-site course and extensive information on the stone used by Crellin. Lastly, I would like to thank my husband Robin L. Armstrong, Professor Emeritus at the University of Toronto, who took many of the photographs and edited the manuscript. For those unfamiliar with the Oxford County farm addresses identified in the figures, the roads run east and west, the lines run north and south. Each farm has a blue sign at the farm gate with the road or the line number in the first two digits followed by a space then the farm address in the last four digits.
2. For further information, contact the author at k.armstrong803@gmail.com.
3. Ruskin, John, 1885, *The Stones of Venice*, New York, John B. Alden, vol. 1, p. 52.
4. Kalman, Harold, 1994, *A History of Canadian Architecture*, vol. 2, Toronto, Oxford University Press, p. 604.
5. *The Canada Farmer*, 1873, vol. 10, no. 1, p. 7.
6. *The Canada Farmer*, 1873, vol. 10, no. 6, p. 98.
7. *The Canada Farmer*, 1873, vol. 10, no. 1, p. 7.
8. Hitchcock, Henry-Russell, 1978, *Architecture: Nineteenth and Twentieth Centuries*, New York, Penguin Books, p. 160.
9. *The Canada Farmer*, 1866, vol. 3, no. 2, p. 20-21; 1868, vol. 5, no. 2, p. 28.
10. *The Canada Farmer*, 1868, vol. 5, no. 2, p. 28.
11. *The Canada Farmer*, 1869, vol. 1, no. 12, p. 450.
12. Mace, Jessica, 2013, "Beautifying the Countryside, Rural and Vernacular Gothic in Late Nineteenth-Century Ontario," *Journal of the Society for the Study of Architecture in Canada*, vol. 38, no. 1, p. 36.
13. Weir, Scott, 2016, "The Picturesque Gothic Villa Comes to Town: The Emergence of Toronto's Bay-and-Gable House Type," *Journal of the Society for the Study of Architecture in Canada*, vol. 41, no. 1, p. 58-59.
14. *The Canada Farmer*, 1867, vol. 4, no. 12, p. 189.
15. Weir, "The Picturesque Gothic Villa Comes to Town," p. 59.
16. Wadsworth, Unwin and P.L.S. Brown, 1876, *Topographical and Historical Atlas of the County of Oxford, Ontario*, Toronto, Walker & Miles, n.p. Crellin is listed as a builder and contractor.
17. Ruskin, *The Stones of Venice*, p. 51.
18. 1841 English Census.
19. Mather, Ian and Margaret Crellin, London, England, private communication, November 30, 2012. Thank you.
20. Wadsworth and Brown, op. cit. The date 1869 is given for Crellin's arrival in Canada.
21. McCormick, Veronica, 1968, *A Hundred Years in the Dairy Industry 1867-1967*, Ottawa, Dollico, p. 11-14.
22. *The Canada Farmer*, 1872, vol. 4, no. 11, p. 403.
23. "Suburban Villa or Farm House," *The Canada Farmer*, 1864, vol. 1, no. 9, p. 132.
24. Upton, Dell, 1984, *Pattern Books and Professionalism: Aspects of the Transformation of Domestic Architecture in America 1800-1860*, Chicago, University of Chicago Press, p. 144-149.
25. "A Cheap Farm House," *The Canada Farmer*, 1864, vol. 1, no. 22, p. 340.
26. "A Two Story Farm House," *The Canada Farmer*, 1865, vol. 2, no. 8, p. 116-117.
27. "A Cheap Country House," *The Canada Farmer*, 1868, vol. 5, no. 16, p. 244-245.
28. "Design of a Small Farm Dwelling," *The Canada Farmer*, 1871, vol. 3, no. 1, p. 16.
29. Downing, Andrew Jackson, 1859, *The Architecture of Country Houses*, New York, Appleton, p. 300.
30. Ruskin, John, 1989, *The Seven Lamps of Architecture*, New York, Dover, p. 77.
31. Naismith, Robert J., 1985, *Buildings of the Scottish Countryside*, London, Victor Gollancz, p. 84-85.
32. Mackenzie, Hugh, 1953, *The City of Aberdeen*, Edinburgh, Oliver and Boyd, p. 230-231.
33. Ruskin, *The Seven Lamps*, p. 83.
34. Id., p. 81.
35. Id., p. 137.
36. Id., p. 24.
37. Hitchcock, *Architecture: Nineteenth and Twentieth Centuries*, p. 248.
38. Henderson Floyd, Margaret, 1997, *Henry Hobson Richardson: A Genius for Architecture*, New York, The Monacelli Press Inc., p. 12, 50, 251.
39. Robert Watt, master stonemason, private communication, April 13, 2015.
40. Meeting with Robert Montaque, July 10, 2014. Thank you for showing me Crellin's Aberdeen Bond barn foundation on the 13th line, no. 6332, Oxford County.
41. Nancy and Victor West, thank you. Their 1883 brick house located just north of the Towle house has a stone foundation built by Crellin.
42. *The Canada Farmer*, 1873, vol. 10, no. 6, p. 98. A quote from A.J. Downing.
43. See Tausky, Nancy Z. and Lynne D. DiStefano, 1986, *Victorian Architecture in London and Southwestern Ontario, Symbols of Aspiration*, Toronto, University of Toronto Press.
44. Id., p. 162-165.
45. Id., p. 177-179.
46. Id., p. 163, 164, 178.
47. Id., p. 83-86.
48. Downing, *The Architecture of Country Houses*, p. 181. Floral motif: the Towle house. Fish scale design: the David Lawrence house and the Alexander Sutherland house.
49. Ruskin, *The Seven Lamps*, p. 5, 20-21, 169-170, 174-175.
50. Private communication with Robert Kordyban, 2012, Thamesford, Ont, Thank you.
51. *The Canada Farmer*, 1873, vol. 10, no. 6, p. 98.
52. *The Canada Farmer*, 1868, vol. 5, no. 16, p. 244-245.
53. Arthur, Eric and Thomas Ritchie, 1982, *Iron: Cast and Wrought Iron in Canada from the Seventeenth Century to the Present*, Toronto, Buffalo, London, University of Toronto Press. Heater with oven (p. 181) is the same as the one in the Lawrence house which was probably delivered to the door by Eaton's.
54. Ruskin, *The Stones of Venice*, p. 8.
55. I would like to thank Ken Judge, owner of the Alexander Sutherland house, and Gordon Whitehead, who lived there in the 1950s, for their assistance in figuring out how the house interior looked in 1891.
56. *The Canada Farmer*, 1864, vol. 1, no. 9, p. 132.
57. Tausky and DiStefano, *Victorian Architecture in London*, p. 86-87.
58. Id., p. 97.
59. *The Canada Farmer*, 1868, vol. 5, no. 16, p. 244-245.
60. Lawrence, David, "How the New House Was Built," *American Agriculturist*, 1894, New York, vol. 53, no. 7, p. 375-376.
61. Ibid.
62. *The Canada Farmer*, 1864, vol. 1, no. 9, p. 132.
63. Reiff, Daniel D., 2000, *Houses from Books, Treatises, Pattern Books, and Catalogs in American Architecture, 1738-1950: A History and Guide*, The Pennsylvania State University Press, University Park, Pennsylvania, p. 133.
64. Tausky and DiStefano, *Victorian Architecture in London*, p. 96-97. For the George T. Mann company, see the map titled: "City of London, Canada, With Views of Principal Business Buildings," Toronto, Toronto Lithographing Co., 1893. Among the businesses illustrated is the George T. Mann company (located at the corner of York and Burwell Streets, adjacent to a major rail line), which, in addition to coal, coke, wood, plaster, and fire brick, also sold Portland cement: [https://ir.lib.uwo.ca/mdc-London-maps/1], accessed August 21, 2018.
65. *American Agriculturist*, 1894, New York, vol. 53, no. 7, p. 375-376.
66. *The Canada Farmer*, 1867, vol. 4, no. 4, p. 60.
67. *Woodstock Evening Sentinel Review*, 1898, three articles of January 8.
68. *Woodstock Evening Sentinel Review*, 1893, February 27, March 6, March 13, March 14, March 20 (all signed with the initials "D.L.").
69. Lawrence, "How the New House Was Built," p. 375-376.
70. *Woodstock Weekly Sentinel Review*, 1904, November 10.
71. Ibid.
72. I would like to thank Lisa Bicum and Geoff Ellis, owners of the Lawrence house, for giving me copies of all the information they have on their house (given to them by the Lawrence family).
73. *American Agriculturist*, 1894, New York, vol. 53, no. 7, p. 375.
74. Hugh McVittie, a David Lawrence grandson, private communication, July 10, 2014.
75. Kornwolf, James D., 1986, *In Pursuit of Beauty, Americans and the Aesthetic Movement*, Museum of Modern Art, New York, Rizzoli International Publications, p. 340-384.
76. Upton, *Pattern Books and Professionalism*, p. 142.
77. *American Agriculturist*, 1894, New York, vol. 53, no. 7, p. 376.
78. Ibid.
79. Ibid.
80. Ibid.
81. Id., p. 375-376.
82. *The Sidney Mail*, 1894, Sidney, Australia, October 20. My thanks to Robin E. Cooper at the University of Guelph.
83. Ruskin, *Seven Lamps*, p. 5, 20-21, 169-170, 174-175.

www.ingramcontent.com/pod-product-compliance
Lightning Source LLC
Chambersburg PA
CBHW052343100426
42738CB00051B/3319